Harasshole

Copyright © Lisa Bowman, 2022

Hardback ISBN: 978-1-957084-03-9
Paperback ISBN: 978-1-957084-04-6
eBook ISBN: 978-1-957084-02-2

All rights reserved. No part of this publication may be reproduced, stored in a retrieval system, or transmitted, in any form or by any means, electronic, mechanical, photocopying, recording, or otherwise, without the prior permission of the publishers.

Foreword

When I began my career as a broadcast journalist, I was the narrator of the story and sometimes the author. I was and am still motivated with the opportunities afforded by my role to share stories. Perhaps the story I share informs someone on a critical issue, helps a decision at hand to be made or in some cases serves as simple entertainment. Stories have the propensity to change lives, one person at a time.

I never envisioned back then that one day, *I* would be the subject of a story that I could not tell.

In July 2016, when I filed my lawsuit against Roger Ailes, I never imagined the power that standing up would carry in inspiring others to step forward with their stories. I certainly did not create the #metoo movement, (thank you Tarana Burke) but I did unintentionally become the public face of it.

I couldn't tell *my* story because of arbitration clauses and the non-disclosure agreement I had to sign, but I could damn well make sure others could tell theirs by working to eradicate those restrictive agreements that serve only to hide toxic behavior. Since then, my purpose, my reason for having gone through this is to mitigate the chances of others not being able to share their stories.

Today, through my organization LiftOurVoices.org, our goal is to protect American workers by eradicating the laws and business practices that prevent employees from publicly discussing and disclosing toxic workplace conditions including harassment and retaliation. It is the ability to share stories, though not my own, that help in advocating for legislation to change these restrictions.

These stories need to be told, if only one at a time, to ensure they are brought into the light and not hidden in the shadows. Though I was unable to do so, I know how hard it is for the brave women that have stepped forward to share their accounts of being subjected to unacceptable behavior. Doing so comes with risk, both personal and professional. If reading one other person's journey on this path inspires you, comforts you or helps you realize you are not alone, I can assure you the author would feel that risk was worth taking.

What makes this story different is that we hear, and are used to hearing, about these issues every day in every sector, entertainment, sports, the government and corporate America. We haven't heard it much in the Non-Profit sector, and surely, it happens. What rings sad here is that these are the very people who are tasked with doing good for our larger society.

Lisa's story is only one of many and I am proud she had the courage to tell it. I encourage you, if after reading this, you say, or just think, "Oh, yeah... #Metoo" please, lift YOUR voice. For it is only when we join together as a chorus, the song becomes too loud to ignore.

Gretchen Carlson
Co-Founder Lift Our Voices, Female Empowerment Advocate, Journalist, Author

To Mad-Dog. You are a brilliant, beautiful girl; I can't wait for the world to experience you. My hope is that you will experience it differently than I did because bad behavior in the workplace will be a thing of the past.

Author's Note

Because there is still a pending legal case surrounding the events that occurred at United Way, I have not included any names other than those that have been publicly used and referenced in media coverage on this issue, or those who have granted me permission. My intent in writing this book is to give an accurate depiction of my experience in the hopes that it will help just one other person who is subjected to what I was. The events cited in this book are derived from my legal documentation (which was submitted under penalty of perjury), other notes, and my memory. Any errors are simply that and not an attempt to change the reality of what took place.

For there is always light if we're brave enough to see it.
If only we're brave enough to be it.
— Amanda Gorman

Harasshole
[hə'ras hōl]
Noun.

Used pejoratively to refer to a contemptible person who creates an unpleasant or hostile environment most often in the workplace with repeated occurrences of uninvited and unwelcome verbal or physical conduct.

Prologue

"You've always had the power, my dear. You just had to learn it for yourself."
—Glinda the Good Witch to Dorothy in
The Wizard of Oz

I never set out to write this book. I wasn't sure I even wanted to. I'm not a celebrity. I don't have all the answers. But then again, this is a story which I have thought hard and long about.

My story, unfortunately, is one that happens EVERY DAY—to thousands of women; and men. It is a story about being silenced and those who have been relegated to silence for a wide variety of reasons, whether by choice or not.

In my case, I had to break the silence. I had to speak up. Typical for me, as I am one who is rarely at a loss for words. This experience, though, may have been the one time I was—or nearly was. It's not that I wasn't afraid; I was unquestionably terrified. But more than that, I was enraged. Furious.

What happened to me was wrong. I couldn't just look the other way and let it go unchecked. I have no regrets. I spoke up for those who endured the same thing I did at United Way but couldn't speak up; because they were either scared or silenced. If I used my voice to speak up, could I also inspire and empower others to do so as well? That is why I spoke up in the first place. If I could perhaps help just ONE single person find their voice, then raising mine was worth it.

As the saying goes, "nothing worth doing comes without risk." And I took that risk.

Personally. Professionally. Because, like Dorothy, I had the power. I just had to learn it. And I hope you do, too.

Introduction

I am a big believer that experiences mean nothing if you don't learn from them. When this experience chose me, it offered me the opportunity to learn and educate others on the hard reality: if you don't speak up for yourself, sadly, nobody will do it for you.

In the pages that follow, I recount my experience at United Way and I want you to know from the very beginning of this story, that should you find yourself in this position, there is obligation and action on both sides, either as an employee or an employer—this should never be forgotten.

Amidst recurring reports of workplace harassment, along with the by now predictable failures of many companies to respond appropriately, it's understandable that employees end up feeling helpless and more likely to give up rather than stand up and fight, concluding that self-protection and silence in an effort to preserve their careers are the smartest courses of action.

I believe the answer to toxic leadership and the environment of harassment that continues to plague the workplace is to fight back, not give up. Such behavior must not be normalized through silent acceptance. Courageously speaking up about injustice or harm may not always help, and it certainly creates personal risks to those who do it. But one thing is certain: remaining silent in the face of injustice will not create a better and more equitable world devoid of this behavior.

Chapter 1

"We realize the importance of our voices only when we are silenced."
Malala Yousafzai

Lisa's House
Atlanta, GA
Monday, November 23, 2020
Around 4 a.m.

"Good news, Lisa, my editor loved the piece! They are going to run it on Monday," explained the journalist from the *Huffington Post* that Friday afternoon.

I could not believe it. It was both terrifying and exhilarating. In just forty-eight short hours, my story would be released to the public. My own little "shot heard round the world" was about to be fired. It would be another critical piece in my effort to shine the light on what was occurring in the workplace and would hopefully draw public attention to prevent it from happening time and time again to employees like me.

Even after all that had happened up to this point, I still could not believe that I was even in this position. I certainly did not intend or even endeavor to become an activist for employees' rights in the workplace. Nevertheless, given how shocking it is when a rare female executive fights back against a high-profile brand like United Way, I was also not surprised when the media expressed interest in the story. Just thinking about this as I learned that the *Huffington Post* article was happening, a vivid flashback washed over me about the day at the office when my boss told me I was "no longer needed." Even though the pages have flown off the calendar since then, at that moment, it felt like it was yesterday.

And yet here I am... 4:07 a.m., and now it is just hours away....

Lying in my bed, I blink, look at the neon green numbers on the alarm clock again, and roll back over. I'd been awake the entire night, staring at the ceiling. I was so tired, exhausted; the adrenaline rushing through my veins and the nervous energy made any chance at sleep impossible. My mind was racing, analyzing all the different potential outcomes.

Would I be strong enough to withstand all the social media trolls and negativity that might come my way? Would people surprise me and actually be supportive?

I reassured myself that I was doing this for all the right reasons: I needed to get the word out, stop this from continuing to happen, and even if I helped just one person, it would be worth it. The months of harassment I had endured at United Way had to stop....

I'd already given up on sleep for the night. I wanted to get out of bed, but there was no reason to. It was eerily quiet in the house. I heard my dog, Mojo, rustling in his bed next to ours. The sounds of the night had always been a comfort to me, even as a child, but tonight they were not able to coax me to sleep. I took a deep breath and soaked in the sounds of the creek running alongside the house, gently tumbling over the rocks in its course. An early-riser frog was croaking his welcome to the morning light that was starting to creep over

Chapter 1

the horizon. The leaves were rustling in the gentle breeze of a cool start to the day. I was reluctant to move—I didn't want to wake my husband sleeping peacefully beside me. I kept thinking, hoping, praying that this was all just a bad dream. The kind where you tell yourself inside your subconscious, "Wake up so this nightmare will be over!" The type that sticks with you even after you're awake and continues to shade the day until you figure out some way to shake it off.

My current problem: I was already awake. As much as I willed this to be a bad dream, it wasn't. It was real. I was still mourning the loss of my dream job and had not yet come to grips with why this had occurred. I had spoken the truth; I had been honest. The research was done. The facts had been checked. I knew in my heart that I had not done anything wrong. Why the hell did I feel so guilty? As if I was the bad guy. I looked down to find that I was clutching a fistful of cotton sheets balled up in my hand. They were the high thread count sheets that I loved. Squeezing that soft fabric was my futile attempt to find comfort in my angst. Having my story validated by the release of the *Huffington Post* article was no cause for celebration. My stomach had been in so many knots for days I would have made a seasoned sailor proud. Over the past couple of days, I had experienced many emotions, ranging from uncertainty to confusion, to fear and anger—all mixed in one terrible mass. All, except joy—joy did not come into play.

4:14 a.m. Less than an hour before I have to get up anyway. I kept repeating in my head that I had done the right thing. Even though there was no turning back now, I still needed to reassure myself that I was following my own beliefs and values. If there's one thing I know, it's myself. After all, we've spent the past half a century together. This time I felt as though I was standing up for something universally wrong, and not just *The World According to Bowman* wrong. And thus, this time, I stood up—on stilts—and I shouted at the top of my lungs from the proverbial rooftops. Lives would be changed after today. Mine already had been. Irrevocably.

Did I make the right decision?

Very quickly, I realized I was starting to hyperventilate—breath in, breath out. I gradually slowed my breathing as I tried to keep my nerves in check.

I glanced back at the clock, 4:27 a.m. My stomach churned, and I fought back the hot tears in my eyes. DO. NOT. CRY. AGAIN.

I must have drifted off for what seemed like only a moment because I woke up to the alarm clock screaming at me. I shut the alarm off, put on my slippers, and headed towards the kitchen to start the coffee machine. My heart skipped a beat as I saw a text message appear.

There it was. The link to the news article. It was live.

Chapter 2

"Be yourself; everyone else is already taken."
Oscar Wilde

I grew up in the Chicago suburbs and was the type of kid who always had a plan. I enjoyed being the one in charge, which even included "managing" my little brother, Jason.

For all of my desire to be a girl who runs the world (thank you, Beyoncé), I was also the kid who never opened her mouth in class and dreaded being called upon by the teacher. Today, nobody ever believes that I was too afraid to speak up in elementary school—especially after "being the UPstander for harassment at my workplace," but I swear, it's the honest truth.

I was always about having a plan and leading others to follow it. Until one day, I unexpectedly found myself without a plan and a pink slip in my hand for standing up for what I believe in. But I'll get to that... soon.

Whether it was urging, okay, railroading, my fellow Girl Scouts into accepting my cookie-selling strategies, or convincing my parents to let me adopt any swimming, flying, or walking creature I brought home with me as long as they had fewer than two or no more than four legs. Thanks to my persuasion skills, over the years, we owned dogs, parakeets, white mice, and a hamster named Bagel, the Houdini of rodents. Bagel could escape from anywhere.

Once, he even ate his way through an encyclopedia placed on top of his cage to keep him from lifting the top off.

However, as a kid, sometimes my plans would backfire. When Jason and I were around four and seven, I decided that before dinner at my grandparent's house for the Jewish holidays, we should get Good Humor Drumsticks from the local ice cream truck and convinced my brother to join me. As I kept watch for adults, Jason darted across Illinois Street, and a car came around the corner, hitting him. Jason was hospitalized with broken ankle bones. That Yom Kippur, I asked for a lot of forgiveness.

I suspect that my planning gene might have been passed down from my maternal grandmother, Libbeye, who passed away in 2015 at age ninety-seven. She was a remarkable woman who took liberal arts classes in 1937, at a time when most women did not finish high school, much less attend college.

Her teachings were common sense but brilliant. One piece of sound advice I still practice every day: "You have two ears and one mouth—use them in proportion." You learn so much by listening; it makes you smarter when you speak.

My mom, Lesley, was the very picture of a warrior. She married my dad shortly after they graduated from the University of Illinois. After I was born, her job was "mom" for a while. But the apple doesn't fall far from the tree. Just like me, she was restless and had a passion for fashion. A former medical assistant, she opened a resale shop called Second Thoughts, filled with a mid-seventies vibe, disco music, wood paneling, and fitting rooms with beaded curtains.

When I was eleven, my parents divorced, and my mom returned to the workforce as a fundraiser and event planner for the March of Dimes and later as District Sales Manager for Budget Rent A Car. Despite a lack of formal education or

Chapter 2

prior experience for either of those jobs, her big personality and can-do attitude got shit done.

I had decided ever since I was a little girl watching my mom in meetings in a big downtown office conference room that I wanted to be a boss with a BIG J.O.B.

My dad owned an advertising agency, and I "interned" for him during summers while in high school. I absolutely fell in love with marketing and the creative world. I was passionate about sitting with the creative team in the "Art Department" while they discussed products and ideas. I watched as concepts came alive on hand-drawn storyboards.

To this day, I call my dad for guidance on advertising and media, including social media! Being in his seventies didn't stop him; he was active on Facebook and even met his girlfriend on Match.com.

Since I was a little girl, I've loved the *Wizard of Oz*. Dorothy's red shoes were #goals. Those red, sparkly heels gave her just a touch of magic and confidence because she knew that if she clicked them three times, she'd go home to her safe place. Back then, I didn't know how much I would someday wish I could click my heels as a method of escape.

While I like to believe that I gravitated towards Dorothy's confidence, perhaps the red shoes foreshadowed an early interest in my lifelong passion for fashion. I wore my first pantsuit at age five: it was pink and from Neiman Marcus. I loved dressing up and never needed an occasion to do so. *The Preppy Handbook* ruled my personal runway in the early eighties; Izod and Polo shirts with flipped-up collars, Levi's pressed with a crease, and penny-loafers. When I first heard a song by Madonna, out went my polos and loafers, in came rubber bracelets, acid washed jeans, and the worst hair I've ever had. Whatever the current trend was, I was down for it.

At five feet tall (only if I stand up straight and fluff my hair), I had already embraced heels by my late teens. While cocktail waitressing in college, I could wear heels while holding a tray loaded with drinks over my head and walk through a crowded room without skipping a beat. To this date, there is nothing I cannot do in five-inch heels. Little did I know they'd become the platform upon which I would stand and the mechanism that would allow me to stand up so that I could stand up for others. It must be true because that's what my Twitter profile says.

My childhood was fairly normal, along with my parents' separation, their failed reconciliation attempt, and then the final divorce, which seemed to be the case with so many other families at the time.

Chapter 3

"I'm tough, ambitious, and I know exactly what I want. If that makes me a bitch, okay."
Madonna

As I entered my teen years, with those early-stage puberty hormones ruling my life, high school was, in many ways, rather forgettable. My parents had divorced by then, and my dad moved to downtown Chicago in a luxury high-rise with a pool and a doorman!

I loved my mom, but the teenage girl-mom dynamic spiraled out of control. During an argument over some mundane issue, I blurted out, "I want to go live with Dad!" She called my bluff and offered to help me pack. I never expected that she would really let me go, but when she did, while my feelings were hurt, onward I went. My brother Jason stayed with my mom in the suburbs, and I headed off for life in the big city.

As I began my freshman year at Lane Tech High School, I was very excited at the prospect of this glamorous new life in the city. My school had 5,000 students from all walks of life, with a freshman class of 1,500. Originally an all-boys school, the imposing Tudor Gothic style four-story-high brick building with its arched entrances situated at the intersection of the busy West Addison and North Western streets looked like a college campus. It had a big football stadium and a sprawling campus where students would hang out on the expansive lawn, on the steps, or in the wide hallways, all filled with the energy of thousands anxious to prove themselves and find their tribe.

In contrast to the city, I grew up in a fairly non-diverse suburb, so meeting people from all backgrounds was amazing. I wanted to soak up their cultures, backgrounds, and life experiences that were so different from mine. Yes, we had similarities; we were all teenagers, some had divorced parents and siblings like me, but they were somehow much more sophisticated since they had grown up in the city. I was anxious to learn as much as I could from everyone: who they were, where they came from, and why they perceived things the way they did.

I am fascinated by people and am always eager to learn what makes someone who they are. I will talk to a rock, and if it talks back, that's a bonus. Everybody, even those with whom you may have nothing in common, has something to share that's interesting or of value. There have been people along the way whom I may not have been able to relate to, but I'm sure I learned something from them. Discover things from those around you and store them away in your toolbox. Moving to the city allowed me to do this, and the experience of being in such a diverse environment stoked my love for travel; it made me want to see the world and find out what it had to offer.

My first opportunity to travel internationally was in my senior year in high school when I took a trip to France with my French class. Visiting Notre Dame Cathedral with its centuries of history, gazing up at the Eiffel Tower, eating the local food—the pastries, the bread, the cheese (!) was an incredible experience. I think my mom was just as excited about the trip, given that she'd never been to Europe. I was so proud to bring her back a gold charm of the Eiffel Tower, which was so precious to her that we buried her with it.

Chapter 3

With graduation impending, my goal was to study journalism at Northwestern University in Evanston, just north of Chicago. I had a career plan—remember, I always have a plan. After earning my undergraduate degree in journalism, I would go on to earn my MBA and then continue on to law school. I wanted to be a criminal defense attorney, but I also wanted to be a TV reporter who would have the expertise to cover famous legal cases. Think Gloria Allred meets Diane Sawyer. The shy girl who wanted to rule the world would be on TV in her fabulous heels discussing provocative legal cases. What a dream!

There is always a time when the plan doesn't work the way it's intended. Plus, at eighteen, we don't always make wise, rational decisions. Only a fifteen-minute drive from home, my parents were able to show up at Northwestern with no advance notice.

Change of plans: I headed to Drake University in Des Moines, Iowa. Drake has a great journalism school, but Iowa was exactly what you think it is; miles of flat farmland filled with corn and polka-dotted with black and white cows. Surprisingly, there was a large contingency from Chicago, and Kansas City shopping wasn't that far for weekend getaways.... Two years later, I transferred from Drake and headed back home after my sophomore year to attend Columbia College in Chicago, where I could be closer to my mom as she fought a second bout with breast cancer.

I majored in communications and was a good writer. (You be the judge; you're still reading this, aren't you?) I had thought that perhaps I would follow in Dad's footsteps in the agency route. The summer after graduation, I set off to secure a job as a junior copywriter, only to realize, much to my dismay, that I could make more money cocktail waitressing and have my days free to hit the beach and spend time with my mom as she continued her battle with cancer.

I was still looking for my first corporate job while waitressing in my high heels. One of the regulars at the restaurant was a nice guy who worked at a nearby office. I didn't know what he did, but he wore nice suits, was well-groomed, and seemed very polished. As we talked one day, he asked if I had ever thought about working in sales. Honestly, I had not. He worked for an electronics company that manufactured printed circuit boards, the components of the central nervous system for electronic devices.
Fast forward, and I had my first job as an inside sales representative, you got it, selling printed circuit boards. I liked the job and the team, and luckily, didn't have to make a sale, just process orders. I didn't want to simply push papers but to understand the ins and outs of the product, and thus always had questions for the engineers. Curiosity may have killed the cat, but it feeds my soul.

Chapter 4

"I never dreamed about success. I worked for it."
Estée Lauder

At the time, I had a boyfriend whose family lived in Atlanta. His grandfather had been a well-known golf legend, and the family business licensed golf apparel products under his name. He decided to move back to Atlanta to enter the family business, and after a year of long drives back and forth and occasional weekends at the halfway point in Louisville, Kentucky, he convinced me to make the big move to Atlanta.

Aside from going away to college, this was my first chance to move away in search of my own young adult adventure. My mom was sick, and there was a bit of trepidation on my part to leave; what if something happened and I wasn't there? She reassured me I was only a plane ride away and encouraged me to follow my heart.

Initially, moving to Atlanta was an exciting transition but a very different environment. I'm used to the concrete jungle not urban sprawl. In 1992 before playing host to the Olympics, the capitol of the South was lots of connected suburbs and very green. I enjoy food. Good food. Ethnic food. And pizza. It's a Chicago thing. I recall asking my new neighbors where to find a good pizza. Their response was, "Papa John's makes a real good pizza, and you can't go wrong with Olive Garden." No offense to these establishments, but no self-respecting Chicagoan would order pizza from Papa John's or be caught gorging on breadsticks and unlimited salad at The Olive Garden.

    My boss in Chicago kindly reached out to his contacts in Atlanta and paved the way for my next job. I accepted an actual sales role, thinking this was the right next progression in my career. I was excited at the prospects of selling now that I could intelligently explain the "pieces and parts" and help someone understand why they should choose us as their vendor. My accounts would be smaller companies in Georgia, Alabama, and Mississippi, and I'd even get to travel to meet with them! I was excited to travel to those southern states which I had never visited before.

    The week before my start date, I was invited to the office for a meeting. After an hour commute to the far south end of Atlanta, I walked into my future employer's office in a non-descript industrial park. The office was filled with unintentional dated vintage furniture and smelled like stale smoke. My soon-to-be boss greeted me in the lobby in a brown, striped, short sleeve shirt, tie, high-waisted brown polyester pants, and cheap, old shoes. We entered the wood-paneled and popcorn ceilinged conference room. He hitched up his pants and sat down, and avoided any eye contact with me.

    With a nervous cough, in his slow southern drawl, he explained that they'd had some time to think about my fit for the sales role. The rest of the sales reps were men, and they couldn't have a "lady" do this job because all the engineers whom I'd be interacting with were male, and "...here in the south, honey, we often entertain male buyers at certain establishments where a young lady shouldn't go."

Chapter 4

As the meeting dragged on, I was reassured that I would be given a "more suitable" job: managing the customer service ladies. I felt stuck and in shock as I listened to this nonsense. This wasn't the position I had applied for. I didn't want to manage the customer service team. Did I even want to be a part of their team? It didn't feel right, and if it doesn't feel right, it's likely not. Despite being clueless as to my next career move, I trusted my gut instinct and walked away from the stinky office, never looking back. In the words of Dionne Warwick, "Walk on By"—something else is waiting.

Nevertheless, I needed a job, and needed one fast. That something else waiting for me was a temporary role at the Estée Lauder counter at Macy's. I loved makeup, so the job fit the bill. Helping someone feel good about themselves was a divine gift which came with the bonus of being able to try EVERY SINGLE new product, PLUS $250 of free product per quarter. I was in literal heaven. I still faithfully use Estée Lauder lash primer under my mascara.

Most of the time, I enjoyed assisting the customers. However, it was at that counter where I had my first experience with racism. Growing up in Chicago, I was surrounded by people of diverse backgrounds from all around the world. There was no hate in our household. My Jewish grandparents, who had fled Europe, certainly didn't teach my parents not to accept others, and my parents certainly didn't teach us that. Even in my general surroundings, I was fortunate enough not to have been exposed to racism or discrimination.

I can even remember a time back in elementary school when I came to the defense of a friend whom others were making fun of. From my house, it was a short ten-minute walk to school: out of my driveway to the left, down two houses to the corner and another left; two long blocks to

Paul's Convenience Store for a mandatory stop for candy; then another block and a half to Illinois Elementary, a flat, sprawling building with a playground at either end.

We traveled in a pack, stopping to pick up others along the way. One day, as we walked home, Rochelle, a tall girl for her age, referred to Laura as "white trash." Her comment triggered a nerve inside me which I had never felt before. I was taught not to make fun of people for their differences, and without hesitation, I sprung forward and grabbed the back of Rochelle's braid. Given the height difference, I was like Air Jordan in my invisible sparkling red slippers sailing through the sky. I pulled her braid hard enough to take her down and ended up in my first and only physical fight ever to this day.

We rolled around on the front lawn of Doreen's house as the rest of the kids cheered loudly. Doreen's mom ran out to the yard and broke up the fight. Later that evening, I was marched down the block by my mom to Rochelle's house to apologize to her and her parents. Yet, I didn't believe I was the one who owed an apology; she was the one who was wrong for talking about Laura in such a mean way. Nevertheless, I felt like I had earned a symbolic badge of honor in self-esteem that day.

I believed in my heart that someone needed to stand up and protect Laura. She wasn't defending herself, and maybe she didn't feel like she could. Perhaps back then, being from a lower socio-economic bracket made her feel like she didn't have the right to push back. Regardless, this boosted my confidence to know that my voice mattered if I stood up for another.

In any case, back to "Beauty Land" at Macy's. One morning, as the store opened, two older ladies showed up at the counter for make-overs. As I called over our resident

Chapter 4

makeup artist, Crystal, you can just imagine my surprise when one of the women stepped close to me and whispered as Crystal came forward, "We don't want HER to do our makeup. She doesn't know how to work on our skin."

I was dumbfounded. I looked at the ladies, then looked at Crystal, and it hit me. Very loudly, I responded, "Oh, because she's BLACK? She's our best makeup artist. You're lucky to be getting her!" They concocted a not-so-well-thought-out excuse about their schedule and left in a hurry.

Hurt for Crystal, I turned to her with tears in my eyes and apologized. "Girl, don't bother. You need to understand you're in the South now. I'm used to it." But that didn't make it okay, and it didn't make me feel any better. I felt like I needed to do something, I just didn't know what that something was.

In retrospect, I now realize that I have a history of standing up for those who have been wronged. It's ironic how hindsight, as they say, is always 20/20, especially as hindsight is what happened to me in 2020. Weird, right?

Chapter 5

"I love to see a young girl go out and grab the world by the lapels. Life's a bitch. You've got to go out and kick ass."
Maya Angelou

While I loved working in cosmetics, I never intended to stay behind the counter for too long. Even though the job was fun, I knew I didn't belong at "Beauty Land." Typically, I go for the natural look with make-up, but I was expected to wear excessive amounts of what I was selling.

One day early in my tenure there, the regional manager dragged me in the back to notify me that I didn't wear enough makeup. Then, without my consent, she proceeded to give me a full makeover, and by the time she was finished, I looked like a clown! After six months, I couldn't keep my happy clown face behind the counter for much longer.

I moved from make-up to copiers, and although I had absolutely no enthusiasm for sales and probably lacked the skills of a natural salesperson, I nonetheless persisted in finding another sales position with the belief that while I hated it, this was the path I was supposed to follow. There is no right path; it's what's right for YOU.

Random thought: How is it that we can put people on the moon and place a rover on Mars, but we cannot make a copier that doesn't jam?!?

My territory was adjacent to Georgia Tech's campus in Atlanta, back then known as Techwood, and was surrounded by some pretty rough areas. Despite this, I armed myself with a list of leads and a map and drove my little red Mazda MX3 into the proverbial hood, wearing my early nineties business suits with shoulder pads. I must admit that I'm directionally challenged and should have known this was a recipe for disaster. One morning, I headed off early and, no surprise, got lost on my way to a building in which I would make cold calls. I found a neighborhood liquor store, already open at 8:30 a.m., and pulled in to ask directions. What's to be afraid of? I was from Chicago, the Big City, and this was sleepy little Atlanta.

A woman in a short-short skirt and high, high heels stood outside the store, with a makeup job likely applied by the regional manager from "Beauty Land." As I got out of the car, she looked at me with an expression that appeared to question what I was doing poking around in her territory. I felt the urge to justify my presence and explained that I was hoping for some directions. She told me "to take my ass out of this neighborhood in my fancy little suit before something bad happens." I respected that and listened to her guidance; we were just two businesswomen out to make a sale that morning.

The one thing that job taught me was that sales was not the right choice of career for me, regardless of whether it was a "character-building role." I've been told over the years that I am always out there selling. But I don't buy that! I hated selling with every fiber of my being. And I sucked at it.

A friend knew of a couple who owned a business and were hiring for a role in marketing and some inside sales type work for their clothing company, Ambitions. In 1993, after eight miserable months in copier sales, I began working for Ambitions out of the couple's basement home office. My inner Glamazon was excited. New York, be

Chapter 5

damned, I'll have a career in fashion right here in Atlanta! I enjoyed my job and absolutely adored the owners, Sid and Adele. Together as a team, we created a clothing brand called LISA for a large national retailer's private label program.

I worked at Ambitions for seven years, through good times and bad. Sid and Adele became my surrogate family in Atlanta. Adele was diagnosed with cancer for the second time just as my mom passed away from cancer. Shortly thereafter, I also broke up with the guy for whom I'd moved to Atlanta. While, I was home in Chicago dealing with "end of life" stuff with my mom, he was off doing what a loving boyfriend or fiancé shouldn't be.

Adele shepherded me through the painful process of putting my life back together and shared with me a great piece of wisdom as I confided life's difficulties with her: "The only thing that will change is the level of acceptance of what you will put up with." This is true not only for #BoyfriendsBehavingBadly, but for life in general.

To this day, Adele is still my SHE-ro and a very close friend. In her late sixties, she started an online business, even appeared on QVC. And remarkably, now in her eighties, she does CrossFit—I could write a whole book about her.

Unchained from my romantic relationship, I decided to stay in Atlanta. It was time for me to move to a new season in my career and life, and leave my legacy, the LISA brand, with my trusted friends and take a great leap of faith toward something new. I moved on from their Ambitions to pursue mine.

My desire to do more is programmed into my DNA: my mom's strong work ethic was passed down to her from her parents, who had immigrated to the U.S. from Russia and

Poland in the early 1900s. "Poppy" came to the U.S. at age eighteen, spoke no English, and went to work in a shoe store. I loved my grandfather's stories about measuring people's feet with a piece of string to determine their shoe size. His hard work earned him the manager title at the store, and he eventually started a small shoe store of his own, which grew into a chain of stores around Chicago. Growing up, Poppy and Nana drove out to our house in the suburbs almost every Sunday, bearing gifts. I remember his breath smelling like coffee from the gold foil-wrapped hard candies he would enjoy at all hours of the day from the stash he kept in his pocket.

"Gram," not Insta, but my dad's mom, was also a sharp cookie. She took over my grandfather's food distribution business when he was recovering from open-heart surgery. She then worked as a telemarketer offering people Mastercard in the early days of credit cards.

As immigrants, my grandparents knew that the only way to achieve their dreams was through hard work, an ethic my parents instilled into me as well. Financially, we always had what we needed and often what we wanted. If I wanted other things, the only way to get them was to earn them. Thus, at the age of ten, I started babysitting in order to earn extra cash for my indulgences. I was able to make just enough to fund my trips to the mall, splurging on Auntie Anne's Pretzels, clothes, and of course cassette tapes of Shaun Cassidy or issues of Tiger Beat.

In the mid-nineties, armed with my tough work ethic, I entered the internet world. As millions of consumers around the world gained access to the World Wide Web, businesses began exploring opportunities with this new mysterious thing called the internet. My aspirations led me to a dot-com start-up, where I spent a quick fifteen months as the marketing director for a B2B auction company that was acquired (unfortunately not during my employment) by Amazon.

In the "rag trade," as it's known, when a brand, let's say, Ralph Lauren, makes a bad bet on a fashion piece that fails to sell as projected, enter the "jobber," the middleman between a manufacturer and a secondary market retailer. Jobbers purchase the excess inventory at a low price and then re-sell it to the secondary retailer à la the "shopportunity" brought to you by TJ Maxx, Marshall's, and the rest for a higher price.

Launched in the early days of the information age, our model cut out the jobber, selling directly to the secondary retailer via auction-based transactions. And as luck would have it, somehow, we were able to secure a meeting in New York with Ralph Lauren (the company, not the man). It was my first trip to the Big Apple, a city that I quickly grew to immensely love. To this day I refer to myself as a native Chicagoan, an Atlanta resident, and a spiritual New Yorker. I recall spending days creating a PowerPoint presentation that used every font, every color, and every animation tool available. Advice to my younger self: keep it simple.

These were the "good old days" of sky-high valuations as investors poured insane capital into dot-com companies (the more things change, the more they stay the same. Seen the market lately?) During the height of the bubble, the tech company we contracted with recruited me for a hybrid marketing-sales role. You'd think by now, I would have learned not to fall for another damn sales job, but I was drawn to the insanity of the new media age.

The tech company represented all of the craziness that came with the dot-com bubble. Like other dot-coms, we grew from sixty-five to over two hundred fifty employees in less than a year. At our high-rise office with a great suburban Atlanta view, we had pool tables, video games, and beer in the fridge—we just thought we were too cool. I am grateful that the friendships I built there still exist to this day after two decades.

One day, my boss brought me into her office. Looking across the highway from our tenth-floor office window, she pointed, "See that building over there? That's UPS. We need a way in." I said, "Game on, challenge accepted."

With my steel-trap memory, I can effortlessly recall insane details about the people I meet—just do not ask what I had for dinner last night. Networking thus came very naturally to me, and I quickly recalled that one of the girls in the office, Cathy, had at one point mentioned that her boyfriend worked at UPS—there's my in! After months of back and forth and weaving a web of connections, I was finally able to crack open the Big Brown doors, where I scored a million-dollar deal, no less, to consolidate all of the independent department websites that had been developed during the early days of the internet under a single UPS brand.

It is worth noting that culturally, UPS is managed by consensus, meaning that everyone has to weigh in and arrive together at some sort of agreement. Thus, to make a sale like that, I had to build trusted relationships, which didn't come overnight. I also loved being at the UPS offices and spent a lot of time getting to truly know the people there. So much so, in fact, that I was one of a few outsiders invited to hear the bell ring in the corporate office on the day of UPS's IPO in 1999. The bell was used only on special occasions, and receiving an invitation for that was a big deal. There was something about the company and the people who worked there that just felt right. And now, more than twenty years after I joined (and left) the company, the thing that was "right", although we didn't talk so much about culture back then, was in fact the culture. Today, when culture is paramount to employee attraction and retention, UPS *still* has an amazing culture albeit one that's evolved over the years to keep up with the social landscape. They are a leader in Diversity: twenty-five percent of the board of directors is "ethnically diverse" and forty percent of board members are women. The most senior internal leadership, known as the Management Committee, is a team of twelve, inclusive of the first ever female CEO. There are four women and four people of color on the team.

Chapter 6

"Power is not given to you. You have to take it."
Beyoncé

I felt like I was in high school about to call a boy whom I had a crush on. Why was I so nervous? I put my phone down, had a sip of coffee, and took a deep breath. It's just an introductory conversation, right? But in reality, it was more than that. It was the start of a new and scary journey down the yellow brick road to the Royal Palace of Oz. Was I really going to do this?

Up to this point, the process of initiating this appointment had been very quick, transactional, and lacking in any real human empathy or emotion: complete a couple of forms online, speak with a paralegal to give some basic details, review the payment terms with an assistant, etc.... But here I was now on the phone about to have that first call with the attorney. After a couple of rings, I heard a very deep, gruff voice answer the phone, "This is Jack!"

Perhaps I was unknowingly speaking my future into existence when in October of 2019, just months before my illegal termination, I had met with a former colleague of mine from UPS, who had previously been an employment attorney. I shared with her what my colleagues and I were experiencing at *America's Favorite Charity* and asked if she was able to recommend some fierce power lawyers who specialized in this area. My qualifying question was succinct, "In all your years of doing this for the corporate side, who were you most afraid to go up against?"

Now, after a ten-minute, anticlimactic conversation, I heard one sentence that made me feel justified and empowered. My new attorney very dryly stated, "I believe this is a case of harassment and even more so, retaliation; we should proceed forward."

To this day, I do not know why it affected me so much, but just hearing those words was a wave of relief. The next wave was filled with EEOC paperwork and strategic discussions. In hindsight, after consulting my attorney, I learned that I had made so many mistakes along the way. For example, I did not file a claim for retaliation while I was still employed. In my many conversations with groups of women regarding sexual harassment that I have today, that is my first piece of advice; know your rights, know the steps (I'll get into that later...).

Chapter 7

"You don't have to play masculine to be a strong woman."
Mary Elizabeth Winstead

In the course of cultivating that big sale to UPS, I had the opportunity to meet high-level executives. UPS had just started up a corporate incubator to leverage the company's IP, infrastructure, and various assets to build dot-com businesses with the intent of spinning them off. They needed people who knew the start-up space and had worked with the venture capital community. Check the boxes, been there, done that.

When one of the executives approached me about joining UPS, my initial reaction was to laugh out loud; when I realized he was serious, I listened. Yes, the offer was interesting, but I didn't fit the culture.

Working for a dot-com, our attire was casual, to say the least: jeans, t-shirts, tennis shoes. I dressed up a bit more business-like than the rest; mostly jeans with high heels because that's just how I roll. In contrast, UPS's dress code was business professional and formal all the way. They wore suits to the office, I loved my jeans. I bought two brown suits to rotate for my meetings with UPS, but that was it. "...As long as I've got my suit and tie—all pressed up in black and white...." Thanks, Justin Timberlake.

With a bit of convincing, I decided to interview. I wore one of my lucky brown suits, with heels of course. After the interview, I didn't need much persuasion and joined UPS in April of 2000 as the Vice President of Market Development for UPS e-Ventures. My first day at work was exhilarating. I proudly pulled into the huge parking garage and took the elevator down to the lobby. The building was elegant, with lots of open, bright space and highly curated art installations throughout the H-shaped building—two towers connected by a bridge. There was even a gym—with classes—and a cafeteria—with a Starbucks!

As I badged in as an official employee, security greeted me on the ground floor with the usual kind smile that brightened my morning. By the end of my first day, my overloaded brain was so exhausted from the joy I had experienced during the day that I simply couldn't recall where I had parked the car that morning. Did I just lose my car in the garage? So much for my steel-trap memory.

The corporate reality of a Fortune 50 came at me hard and fast. Initially, I had no clue how to navigate through UPS's powerfully ingrained culture. My boss had been there forever and a day and, like so many others, started as a part-time loader in college, becoming a driver, and then was sent up to Corporate. He knew all the tricks. I quickly learned that much of the business got done in the cafeteria; the only spot where coffee was allowed in the building, and began to schedule coffee meetings with others to get stuff done. I had asked my boss for a list of people with whom I should set up coffee meetings and asked each of them to introduce me to two or three others whom I should meet. Very shortly, my web of connections exponentially grew within the company, and I had the privilege of meeting amazing individuals over coffee.

I was a bit of a unicorn at UPS in those days, a rare mythical creature: young, female, and an outsider—the

Chapter 7

cardinal sin. I was often the only woman in meetings among ten to twelve men more senior to me, whose entire careers were at UPS. At that point, I believe the average tenure of a UPS employee was twenty-eight years! Holy brown shorts, Batman!

Speaking of the brown shorts, roughly six weeks after I started, Human Resources informed me that I was scheduled to attend "District Experience," a training program for new hires, usually college age, that placed them into one of the sixty operating districts of UPS to learn operations and the business. I was pumped.

When my boss found out, he hit the ceiling. "There's no way you're going to do that," he thundered. He was a big, loud, rough guy and, as I'd soon come to find out, was not only best friends with Captain Morgan but lived like him, too.

Not understanding the rationale behind his response, I begged and pleaded endlessly to attend. At UPS, time really is more money; efficiency in time and space meant more packages delivered faster. However, I knew that I had to learn the operations. I needed the "District Experience," since not having come up through the operation was a huge deficit. UPS stood for United Parcel Service, and I needed to understand how a parcel was serviced before I would be able to pitch my new "out of the box" ideas to a room full of fifty-plus-year-old men with decades of operational experience.

To this date I'm still not sure how I managed to convince my boss to sign off for the training, but off I went to Orlando, Florida that June to work in operations for two and a half weeks. I proudly ordered my uniform to wear when I was "on car"—you NEVER refer to a UPS vehicle as a truck; they are package cars.

The UPS employees in the local operation thought I was a total freak, rightfully so—I was absolutely ecstatic to wear the uniform and learn every possible task I could: loading and unloading the cars, riding with a tractor-trailer driver, answering calls in the customer service center, going on sales calls, and even learning how time studies were conducted.

The first day I was "on car," we were in a mobile home community. I proudly trotted up the driveway with the QVC package tucked under my arm. A woman answered the door as I rapped on it and called out, "UPS." She looked at me quizzically and said, "Well, aren't you the cutest lil' UPS thing. I don't think I've ever seen a girl deliveryman. Honey, on behalf of me, and Oprah and all the rest—thank you!" I thanked her politely and held my laughter until the end of the driveway.

As we were wrapping up the day, our delivery route took us out to a more rural area. We pulled into a long narrow driveway. As I started towards the house, I heard a growling that sounded like an enormous creature, and out of nowhere, a monstrous dog came charging at me. Shit! What did the training manual say about beast attacks? What was it that I was supposed to do again?

For a split second, I dove into freeze mode, quickly followed by the flight response. Possibly breaking Usain Bolt's record as I lunged quickly for the car door, the beast almost knocked me over as it skidded to a stop right in front of me and rolled over for a belly rub. I looked back to find the driver with whom I was riding doubled over with laughter; she knew. This still puts a smile on my face even to this day.

Besides the dog incident, I immensely enjoyed my time "on car." At Corporate, it was easy to sit behind a desk in the office and lose sight that the real business going on was "out there" with the drivers. Every year, I dedicated at least a day "on car" and encouraged my team members to follow suit.

In a company whose operations are highly dependent on safety, the five-inch heels were a dead giveaway that I was from the *outside*. UPS had a strict corporate dress code. And, while I preferred skirts and dresses over pants, initially, in this very male dominated environment, I unconsciously drifted to wearing only pantsuits and plain white or blue blouses to blend in with the crowd. I felt uncomfortable standing out, and I felt that if I wasn't noticed, the men wouldn't label me as "the woman." I changed who I was, how I showed up, just so I wouldn't feel different. This was my "corporate camouflage," and once I realized the path I was on, I reunited with the skirts and dresses collecting dust in my wardrobe and quickly reverted to my true self. Why is it that WE (us women) feel that we are the ones who have to change, rather than just being agents of change?

One of my hallmarks at UPS—and anyone who knows me can vouch for this—was my shoes. Always high heels; I never met a pair of Pradas I didn't like. Heels are the logo of my personal brand.

There was the time I was in a New Jersey operations facility conducting a focus group with drivers. My friend Paul, who managed the operations center there, was on vacation that week and had offered me his office in his absence. The following week, he called to say, "You are NEVER to step foot in my operation again." Oh my gosh, what did I do? I had cleaned up after myself and made sure to lock the door as instructed. "Paul, I'm so sorry," I apologized. He started laughing. "You totally ruined my drivers. They aren't used to a female in a skirt and heels in the building, and that's all they've been talking about. Did you seriously walk through my center in five-inch heels?" he asked me incredulously. Guilty as charged!

While I loved UPS and my career there, I was in a never-ending silent, unspoken battle with my boss. The man was fond of "team bonding," which meant meeting up at a bar near the office at 5:30 p.m. to hang out, while he typically drank nearly an entire bottle of rum.

At first, I felt pressured to enlist with the legion, even though I didn't want any part of this. More than once, I faked a call from home as an excuse to leave early, but when I stopped showing up at all, his voicemails began.

"You're just a stuck-up bitch that won't hang out with us because you think you're better than we are," he'd slur into my voicemail, totally drunk. At first, I tried to ignore his behavior. But my quiet resistance failed to be effective, and he persisted.

I was young, in my early thirties. I had no experience with this, and back then, sexual harassment training wasn't yet a thing. All I knew was that I did not like where this was heading. Finally, I decided to report his repetitive and unacceptable behavior.

Naively, I spilled my side of the story to the VP of Human Resources. "I don't want to be a problem or get him into trouble," I pleaded. "I just want it to stop." I played a voicemail or two. The VP shook my hand as I walked out of his office, assuring me that he'd handle this delicately and that my boss would be spoken to. Mistakenly, I felt heard and validated.

One of its remarkable qualities is that UPS is like a family; people created incredibly strong, lasting bonds in this workplace, especially if they've come up the ladder together. This was a culture I truly admired. However, what I failed to

Chapter 7

realize was how deep the bonds were, and that my boss and the VP of HR went waaaaay back.

The afternoon of the following day, my boss stormed into my office. My office was situated with my desk facing the door and my chair backing up to a wall. Red-faced with fury, he cornered me against the wall screaming that I was a troublemaker. "You think you can just go to HR on me?" he bellowed.

I was petrified and at a loss for words. I clung to my seat. My boss overwhelmingly invaded my personal space, and I literally had nowhere to go. Calmly, I tried to reason with him. I managed to patch my words together and said, "Please stop screaming and leave my office," hoping my words would interrupt his shouting. "We can speak about this when you calm down," I added, but he kept on yelling and spitting in my face.

Blood was already boiling in my veins, and I didn't want this one-sided fight to erupt into a huge disaster. Terrified, I grabbed my purse, pushed past him, and ran out of the building in tears.

I had no idea what I needed to do next. I still couldn't believe what had just happened. Is this what big company life was all about? At that point, I decided that I should call the VP of HR. Getting his voicemail, I left a message about the incident in my office and that I'd be back in the building in the morning.

The next day, I dreaded going into the office. Soon after I arrived, the VP of HR came to see me. He informed me about a change in my reporting structure. Overnight, I no longer reported to my boss but instead to a peer VP.

What did this all mean? Was I demoted? Drowning in doubt, I tried to comprehend why I was the one being punished here, but in that moment, I didn't care—I was relieved to have the distance between myself and that man. In a company of ~400,000 employees, it's fairly easy not to encounter someone if you don't wish to. I had limited interaction with my former boss after this, and shortly thereafter, he was demoted and subsequently left the company. I don't know the circumstances, but I do know for sure that unethical and inappropriate behavior is not tolerated at UPS. They set the bar high and live up to it. In retrospect, while an unpleasant experience, it paved the way for my next one and all of the wonderful ones there that followed.

Chapter 8

"Determined people working together can do anything."
Jim Casey (Founder of UPS)

In 2001 just over a year after I joined UPS, the dot-com bubble began its burst, and I worried I might soon be jobless as UPS started dismantling e-Ventures. At the time, I was on a technology products repair service project where devices were returned via UPS to its repair facility in Louisville, Kentucky. I heard the project was going to be integrated into another business unit's offerings, and fortunately, I was asked to help with the transition.

Back then, it was inconvenient for customers to return packages. At that time, there were no UPS locations in neighborhoods; you had to go to one of the operating centers, which had a customer counter and were usually located in industrial areas.

During that same year, UPS also acquired the business services franchise MailBoxes, Etc. This was my AHA moment! Why couldn't UPS utilize the newly acquired Mail Boxes, Etc. locations which were already conveniently located in strip malls? My memory may fail me here, but at that point, there was a MailBoxes, Etc. location within five miles of roughly eighty-six percent of the U.S. population.

I "reached out" to the person in charge of integrating the acquisition for a coffee date. In the cafeteria, we quickly moved from discussing my plan to brainstorming about various other opportunities to explore with these new stores.

Things work in mysterious ways at UPS. When I returned to my office in a satellite building, I was called into my boss's office. Apparently, the meeting had gone REALLY well, and I already had a new position in a newly formed team to determine the strategy for the new franchise network UPS had acquired.

The franchise was headquartered in San Diego, and for the next seven years, I commuted to California regularly. San Diego always had the perfect climate, and the office in Cali was cool: a triangular shaped building with open hallways, and the cafeteria made mouthwatering avocado sandwiches. I was responsible for overseeing the marketing, communications, and branding for what eventually became The UPS Store®. I just loved this job.

The UPS Store locations were owned by independent franchisees who invested in a physical location which they owned and access to brand and operating plan from the franchisor. Business owners were a sort of Middle Earth residents; they didn't like the corporate structure because they had their visions on how to run the business in an entrepreneurial spirit. Yet, they weren't sole entrepreneurs since they bought into a franchise with an established brand and an operational playbook they were expected to follow.

We worked endlessly to prepare for the series of pitches to convince the business owners to convert to the UPS brand. We had a solid business case built upon rational points such as expected revenue upside, new customer growth rates, high conversion products, and services that would be provided under the new brand. But, this was also an emotional decision for the franchisees. Initially, they had

Chapter 8

bought into an independent brand and had now been sold to one of the largest companies in the world.

Early on during the process, I visited a store owned by a franchisee who had been vocal about not being a fan of UPS. When I introduced myself, he responded with, "Oh, you're one of the bitches from Corporate." I told him I'd turn around and walk out and be back in five minutes. When I returned, I expected him to show better manners and greet me appropriately. And he did. Take no shit. You don't need to allow people to disrespect you.

At the end of that long day in the store, he recognized that I wasn't the enemy. UPS wasn't trying to do anything nefarious, only to help them be more profitable. We were in this together—we didn't do well if they didn't do well; there was no other motive.

Working with the franchisees, I learned a valuable professional skill: managing through influence. We couldn't dictate the franchisees to accept the new brand as they were not our employees. Some didn't even want to be a part of the UPS family, and I had to learn to win these folks over one at a time in order to create an extensive network of stores operating under a single brand.

In April 2003, two years after the acquisition, we announced the conversion of MailBoxes, Etc. to The UPS Store. Approximately 3,300 franchisees in the U.S.—nearly ninety percent of the domestic network in the U.S—adopted the UPS brand. Victory!

Did I say I loved my job at UPS? For the next five years, I relished every second of my time at work.

Compared to the corporate headquarters, the San Diego office culture was quite different. After all, it was Southern California and super casual, unlike the UPS office back in Atlanta. One day, as I was headed out to San Diego on an afternoon flight, I tempted fate with what I was wearing when I made a morning pit stop at UPS's office to knock out some work. At the time, UPS's dress code still required jackets. Sleeveless tops and open-toed shoes were strictly forbidden. Women were required to wear hosiery—I know, whaaaaaat? That day, and here comes my memory again, I wore a white pantsuit with a pink blouse. I had just bought a cute pair of peep-toe pumps. Only one toe showed. They were white with a stacked wood heel and had multicolor leather dot cut outs: pink, turquoise, green—so adorable! The pants were almost long enough to hide the shoes. Since I would be in the building for less than half a day, I decided to take my chances. I cowered in my cube, too afraid to roam the halls so as not to be busted.

Mid-morning, and of course as fate would have it, the fire alarm went off. Damn it. I scurried down the five flights of stairs to my designated zone in the parking garage. Do you ever have the sense that someone is staring at you and you're almost too afraid to look to see if it's true? The eyes that were on me—sharply, no less—were those of the Chief HR Officer who glared directly at my big toe creeping out from under the hem of my pants. I shuffled uncomfortably and tried to edge behind a colleague, but it was too late. She had already spotted me and my blatant disregard for the corporate policy that stated no toe should ever see the light of day. I mean, come on, I got regular pedicures, and my polish wasn't even chipped. One thing I am a freak about is my nails. I'd rather give up food than a manicure, and you will NEVA EVA catch me with chipped polish. No way, no how. Regardless of the quality of my pedicure, it appeared UPS, and my toes were not going to see eye to eye.

The last time I was at UPS, just a few months ago, people were in jeans. They now allow you to have visible tattoos.

Chapter 8

And, to my surprise, they are on TikTok. With 114 years of history in the rear-view mirror, they've managed to keep the best aspects of things, while continuously evolving to stay relevant. And, I love the fact that the new CEO is female; in 2021, only eight percent (forty-one) of the Fortune 500 CEO's are women. We've got work to do.

Chapter 9

"The future depends on what we do in the present."
Mahatma Gandhi

In 2005 when working on The UPS Store project, I was selected to attend a Community Internship Program (CIP), a month-long community service program. Typically, such programs may be associated with celebrities completing their probation requirements, such as Paris Hilton, who had been photographed doing community service in four-inch heels following a 2010 conviction. That's how I'd do community service, but that's beside the point.

CIP was a pivotal moment in my life. Each year, groups of ten selected executives were sent to one of four locations; McAllen, Texas, the Henry Street Settlement in New York, Chinatown in San Francisco, and a Tennessee community in Appalachia. Each community had a discrete set of issues and challenges they faced. Participants were taken one hundred percent out of their jobs for a month to work in the assigned communities.

Initially, I was slated for New York, but was switched to Texas at the last minute. I was thankful to have a new perspective, as growing up in Chicago, I was already familiar with the inner-city issues of drugs and gangs.

McAllen, on the other hand, was an eye-opener. I was there with eight guys, all operations managers, who all became my brothers by the end of the trip. Paul, who had teased me for wearing five-inch heels in his building, was one of them. The first international participant in the program was Elena, an Italian colleague who did business development. Given the politically different structure between the U.S. and Italy, she didn't understand the whole notion of volunteerism and community service. In Italy, the government would have addressed that, not private citizens.

My residence for the month was a room with an outdoor entrance at a La Quinta Inn hotel that had a heavy truck driver customer base. The rooms were tiny but functional, with old stained wallpaper and a comforter that I was not going to touch. The hotel pool and a HEB grocery store a few blocks away were a big plus.

The first Saturday of our stay, our hosts and community organizers in McAllen, Mary and Reyes, a lovely older couple, took us to Mexico. I had been invited to attend church with our hosts the following day and had to break it to them that I was Jewish. They looked at me like I had three heads and had told them Jewish people sacrificed goats to the Gods. That Saturday in Mexico, Elena and I were solicited for store-front dentistry and plastic surgery as we walked around the streets of Reynosa. "Hola, Señoritas! New boobies? We do it fast and cheap." No, gracias.

Back then, and presumably still today, there were two groups in McAllen, the snowbirds who had fled south for the winter and the locals. Most of the people we met were of Mexican heritage, and many were likely illegal. We didn't ask, we didn't care, and it didn't matter. The impoverished living conditions were like nothing I'd ever seen. Families had to save up to purchase cinder blocks to construct their homes. I suppose that may not sound like a big deal. The kind of cinder blocks I'm talking about cost $1.77 per piece today. But these were migrant farmers picking produce for under a dollar per hour. Most had no running water. The kids had no shoes to wear to school. However, they were grateful to live in such conditions because this was an improvement to where they came from and presented an opportunity for them and their children.

It was tremendously gratifying to work together as a team, focusing on big projects such as building houses. I am great at cutting out electrical sockets and window frames with a router. I broke a couple of nails as my eye-hand coordination with a hammer wasn't so good. And fortunately, the guys kept me away from saws and other sharp objects.

Other projects were assigned to us based on our individual areas of interest. And to help us select whom we wanted to work with, we each visited a host of non-profits to understand their impact and programs. For example, one of my colleagues wanted to work at a substance abuse facility, as he had grown up with an alcoholic father.

The high-school graduation rate in McAllen was thirty percent. With a permanent population of around roughly 100,000, the best career opportunity some of these high school kids could strive for was a job at the local Walmart. Maybe, IF they were able to graduate high school, they could become a manager at that Walmart one day. And to compound the issues the community was faced with, teen pregnancy and alcohol abuse were rampant.

Rather than choose a single group, I decided to work with several organizations because there was so much I wanted to do. I taught occupational skills to teenagers, showing them how to complete a job application. Don't use purple ink, let's put a dot over the "i" instead of a flower. Use your real name, not what your boyfriend calls you. They also conducted mock interviews with each other and voted on who should get the job, and learned about dressing appropriately for an interview (it's okay to wear jeans if that's what you have, but cover up the belly button ring), shaking hands, and making eye contact.

By the end of a physically and emotionally draining week, we were all looking forward to having a day off. I brought bakery-fresh tortillas and a bag of avocados back to my room while the guys loaded themselves with booze they had bought in Mexico. At about 10 a.m., there was a banging on my door. I was greeted by the guys in their swim trunks announcing, "Pool party at noon." We had the pool to ourselves, and my delicious guacamole made with perfectly ripe avocados was a hit. Needless to say, there was quite a bit of alcohol flowing.

At about three in the afternoon, Mary and Reyes stopped by the hotel to check on us. Displeased with the scene before them, future CIP groups were thus required to stay in a local seminary under their watchful eyes.

Halfway into the program, one of the social workers pulled me aside. There was a family she wanted me to meet. Their tragic story could be a whole book in itself. A widowed father with five young daughters aged fifteen, thirteen, nine, seven, and two, their mom had been killed in a recent car accident with the entire family in the car. The father had been driving, the two-year-old went through the windshield and suffered a traumatic brain injury and would never recover. To provide for the family, the father worked odd jobs and picked in the fields, and had no health insurance.

The social workers asked Elena and me to spend some time with the girls to offer them some female companionship, even perhaps teach the older ones to cook. We agreed to do it, having no clue what we were signing up for.

Chapter 9

In the car on the way out to their house, we teased each other. I didn't cook, but stereo-typing Elena based on her Italian heritage, I was sure she did. In her most indignant English, "Hell no, I don't cook!" she assured me. We decided we'd just figure it out upon arrival. UPSers always do.

Pulling down a long dirt road with nothing but flat dry land around us, we arrived at a trailer located in the middle of nowhere, a few miles from the town. The broken front stairs were hazardous. There was a washing machine outside with tangled up electrical wires and plugs that led to a municipal power pole. That didn't look safe either.

As we got out of the car, the girls emerged and walked shyly towards us. We smiled with the hopes of building trust fast.

The tiny two-bedroom trailer they were living in was in complete disarray, with clutter everywhere. The four girls crammed into a bedroom at one end with double bunk beds, while the father and the toddler stayed in the bedroom at the other end. There was a single bathroom for all. Through the screenless windows, I saw the dog that lived outside, foraging for itself. The filthy dog's visible ribs were heartbreaking.

It didn't take us long after we arrived to learn the full extent of their situation. We were there in April, and the girls were on spring break from school. The only meal they routinely got was the school provided lunch, and the food that had been sent home was almost all gone.

In terms of their clothing, each of the girls owned two pairs of jeans, a couple of pairs of underwear, and a few tops. They were fortunate enough to have a washing machine, but the clothes were hung outside on a line to dry. Elena and I looked at each other in dismay, unsure of what to do. All that we did know was that we needed to do something.

We started talking to the girls, who were bashful and quiet, trying to get them to trust us. We made a game out of cleaning up, looking to see what they had and needed. I could tell that the oldest one was not wearing a bra, which she desperately needed to be. Knowing they had enough food for one more day before we left, we asked if we could come back tomorrow and "play" some more, to which they said yes.

Back at the hotel, we then made our plan. When we reconvened with the whole group later that night, we shared our experience, and the two of us enlisted the guys to help the next day. One of them was from our automotive function. He and another were assigned (by us) to do something, anything, with the washing machine, to make it as safe as possible to use. The others were to fix the stairs and anything else they could. The challenge was to find a way to bring them over and not put the dad in an uncomfortable position. The following day, we showed up and asked the dad if we could take the four older girls out for a bit. With his permission, we headed to Target with the girls to do some shopping.

Elena and I bought clothes, cleaning supplies, and food. The girls didn't know what sizes they wore, and I helped the older one with bras. They also picked out a few "gifts" for their dad. We wanted them to have things they wanted, not just the basics: coloring books, dolls, nail polish. They were like fish out of water. This was a totally new experience for them, and they didn't know how to react. Between Elena and me, we spent about $600, the best money I have EVER spent.

Over the next few weeks, we adopted the family and spent time with them every day. We brought them to the lovely McAllen LaQuinta, our home during the trip, to swim in the pool. Elena and I took them out for their first time in a restaurant, Chili's—the menu overwhelmed them. The idea of being able to order whatever they wanted was unfathomable. We "accidentally" ordered an extra meal for the dad, too. We never wanted to offend him or give the impression that we thought he couldn't take care of his kids. Unfortunately, we learned the hard way that the dad had a drinking problem. He didn't speak any English, but the guys took him out with them one night for burgers and beer. When we mentioned that to the Social Services, they were not pleased.

At the end of CIP, the team received a $1000 donation from The UPS Foundation that we could allocate as a charitable grant to one of the organizations with whom we had worked. We lobbied HARD and got the approval to give it to the family; they needed so much. We allocated it to the service organization who had introduced us to them, and I became the executor of the money they could inquire about when they needed it. We also each added funds to create a $3500 escrow account for them. For years to come, I sent Walmart gift cards and boxes of clothes to the McAllen agency for them. Unfortunately, they did not have a legal mailing address where I could directly contact them. Over time, the people at the agency changed, the money ran out, and I eventually lost contact with them.

I came back from McAllen a changed person. I'd always been quick to write a check (no Venmo back then) for someone in need but had never leaned in and done the hands-on labor.

I also realized that as a marketer, and by my own admission, a good one at that, UPS would be perfectly capable of generating its next billion dollars of revenue with or without me in marketing.

The CIP experience made me understand that I wanted to be a part of a greater purpose, which ultimately started me down the path towards my career at United Way. Yet if I had only known at the time what the ultimate cost would be....

Chapter 10

"Life didn't bring you this far to only bring you this far. The most beautiful part of the journey is just beginning."
Unknown

Upon returning from my uplifting internship, I was armed with a mission to secure a role in The UPS Foundation. I walked down to the Foundation at the UPS headquarters and announced, "Hi. I just got back from my CIP. Thank you for the grant money, and I'd like to work here." The Foundation sent me back multiple times with my tail between my heels.

I quickly learned that there was no fast track to checkmate; that was simply not how UPS functioned. The Foundation, as it is known, sits within the HR function, and I was in Marketing. One could not just switch functions, just as one could not switch families.

The cultural mechanism at UPS reminds me of an epic episode of *Sex and the City* from 2003, called "Great Sexpectations," where Charlotte announces her intentions to convert to Judaism to marry the man she loves. She goes to the synagogue and tells the Rabbi, "I want to become a Jew." Three times he sends her away. He finally allows her in, and the process begins. It took almost five years of endless cups of coffee at the cafeteria before I finally got a break. In the meantime, I continued to enjoy my life at UPS.

One thing I always used to coach my team on was that at UPS, change was a constant. If you loved your job, never whisper it out loud because the minute you did, they'd give you a new one. If you hated your job, don't worry, you wouldn't be there long.

I must have accidentally mentioned out loud how much I loved my job. BAM! Time for a change. As I mentioned, I didn't "grow up" at UPS. My work focused on creating new processes and opportunities, not working with the established core business, which was both a blessing and a curse.

My new role was in product development, and I was assigned to identify adjacent business opportunities outside the core business. I had a small team to work with and resources which were "begged, borrowed, and stolen" from other functional areas that flexed up and down with the phases of the project.

In general, residential deliveries, the packages that come to our homes, are costly for UPS because they lack density. At least pre-Covid. The more packages added to a stop, the more profitable it is. Could we leverage the trust equity in the brand and the delivery capabilities of UPS to create a product line delivered by our drivers and offer value to our commercial clients? This was the birth of UPS Direct to Door.

The concept was quite simple, in theory. UPS would compete with direct mail by delivering coupons, offers, and even samples from our commercial clients while dropping a package to the customer. We'd layer another package onto an existing delivery to drive the overall cost down and help increase the sales for our commercial clients whose products we delivered. It was a win-win for all.

Since our drivers were loved and the brand was trusted, we expected a halo effect that would, in turn, extend to the contents of the promotional package. We'd have a competitive product against the "blue envelope" in the mailbox filled with offers. And, if we only made it available to companies that shipped via UPS, we'd have a competitive value proposition against the "F word" (FedEx). Brilliant in theory if I do say so myself. But could it work operationally? I set off to investigate.

While the concept was different from anything else we'd ever done, it was nevertheless completely aligned with the objective of "adjacent to the core business." We worked with our customers, clients, operations, and tech teams to bring the idea to life. In the end, it all came together. Not easily, though.

As I kept on obsessively exploring a variety of ideas, my boss and others thought that I had lost my mind. Maybe I did. Or maybe my perspective came from a different lens because of my background. Diversity isn't only about the box you check on a form, it also includes different backgrounds, experiences, and an uncommon way of thinking we bring to the table.

Once we built a solid business case, it was then time to present the concept to the "Product Development Committee," PDC, (UPS is famous for its litany of acronyms and had an acronym guide for new employees) for test market approval. PDC included the CEO and several of his direct reports. Needless to say, nobody wanted to fail in a rare presentation in front of this group. These meetings were a BIG DEAL. Scheduled to take place in a specific conference room used for important meetings, I stood in the center of a u-shaped table surrounded by the executives. Undoubtedly, I was nervous, but as I've said, we all put our high heels on the same way, right?

Before the meeting, my boss told me, "Here's the deal, Lisa. If you sink, you sink alone. If you swim, I swim with you." Clearly, he either had an overwhelming sense of confidence in my ability or a real zest for self-preservation—or both. I had prepared as well as one could, trying to anticipate any and every question that could be thrown at me. If worse comes to worst, I was willing to take the risk and sink alone.

During the presentation, the CFO, out of the blue, asked me which customers we had spoken to. I blanked—a total whiteout between my ears. I gulped for a last breath of air. My confidence began to evaporate as I managed to recall only two of the over twenty customers. I was going to sink. Fast. And alone.

At the end of the presentation, dead silence took over the room for what felt like forever. I watched the door expecting security to come remove the crazy girl from the presence of the executive team. Finally, the COO leaned back in his chair with his arms behind his head. He turned to the CEO and said he saw no reason not to proceed with test marketing. The CEO nodded with a smile.

What just happened? My slip-up didn't kill me. We're people; we're not perfect. The truth is that if you mess up a presentation, you are usually the only person that knows it. Remember, the audience doesn't KNOW what you're going to present, that's why they showed up to hear you!

We jumped into the test market phase with both our feet. As with all endeavors at UPS, we measured the results and measured some more, and determined the product to be quite successful. Our test clients included marquee brands like Bed Bath & Beyond, who tested Direct to Door as an alternative to their traditional mailed coupon postcard, as well as Men's Wearhouse. By the end of the test phase, data showed that redemption rates of the Direct to Door offers exceeded those of their traditional direct mail. It appeared

Chapter 10

that we had a winning product that would both reduce cost and generate profitable revenue.

While we were out in the market testing the product, I took the Chicago area. It had been too long since I'd been home. While "on car" eating a Portillo's hot dog I'd talked the driver into stopping for with an offer to buy his lunch, I got a call from our PR team. The *New York Times* wanted to interview me immediately; they were on a tight deadline. I was in my brown uniform riding in a noisy package car, but I did it, background noise and all. Even better, we scored great coverage in the *Times*.

Just as we began to productize Direct to Door in the fall of 2009, the country was in the midst of the housing crisis, and the market was nervous. As a result, customers were apprehensive about allocating already constricted advertising dollars to something so new, even though we had data to back it up. We couldn't get traction quickly enough to bring the product to life. I was profoundly disappointed but also knew that I couldn't control our country's economic environment. This past year, during the Covid quarantine, certainly would have been a great time to resurrect this product. No playing with makeup at Sephora—send a sample. No samples of non-perishables at Costco—send a sample. Oh well, moving on.

Chapter 11

"Do something today that your future self will thank you for."
Anonymous

The following year in 2010, the opportunity that changed the trajectory of my career, and life, knocked on my door. The head of HR and I ran into each other at the elevator. He shared that a little bird had told him I wanted to join the Foundation since my CIP back in 2005. I nodded, and he winked.

When I got the offer, the marketeers were not pleased. One senior manager went so far as to tell me that he hoped I had a successful career in Human Resources because marketing was now "closed" to me. I honestly didn't care.

That October, I joined The UPS Foundation as the Director of Corporate Relations. I also functioned as the Chief Marketing Officer (CMO), even though, on paper, the role didn't exist. My first day on the job came with a gift with purchase: running the company's United Way campaign—my excitement for the new job faded quickly.

United Way, the world's largest non-profit, aligns with corporate America to solicit donations from their employees, often supplemented by a matching contribution from the employer itself. At the time, UPS was the second largest corporate donor to United Way, contributing about $48M annually. As I've said, and will continue to say, I am not good at sales, and this was the worst kind of sale I could be asked to make: soliciting my colleagues for donations.

I recall on my first day at UPS, I was handed a pre-printed United Way pledge form with my name and a suggested donation amount for my level. I was politely told, "We support United Way, and we're sure you will want to as well."

I had no inkling about who United Way was or what they did. But I felt pretty confident that if I failed to complete the form and didn't donate, I would end up on a secret blacklist of the un-promotable. I smiled and softly replied, "Thank you SO much for allowing me to contribute. I'd be happy to."

From that point on, I dutifully contributed to United Way annually without fully understanding who they were, what they did, or why I was giving. You can understand why I was reluctant to oversee this dreaded task; I didn't want to be that person who walked into the cafeteria, and everybody scattered out of fear of me hitting them up for contributions. Perhaps I'm being a bit dramatic, given that it actually wasn't me doing each individual ask, but I was the face for the overall campaign.

As any good marketer would do, even one now branded as an "HR person," I started with a situational assessment and some research. If employees were the target market, how did they feel about the "product," i.e., donating to United Way? What drove their "purchase" decisions? How could I influence them to "buy" or "buy more"?

The problem was not the "product" itself. A survey we conducted revealed that a mere nine percent of our employees felt like they personally knew someone who had benefitted from United Way. Only nine percent; in my gut, that didn't feel right. My hypothesis was that our people felt that United Way helped those nameless, faceless folks outside our own four walls. Yet, I suspected that some

UPSers had themselves even been beneficiaries of United Way. I had the start of a plan!

Each year, one of the Management Committee members served as the Chairperson of the campaign. In my first year, it was the COO, David Abney. The same man who had supported the market test of Direct to Door. I pitched the idea that if more UPSers shared how they benefited from United Way, others would realize that United Way helps everyone, perhaps even the person on the other side of their cube wall. His response was that he felt UPS employees were perhaps too proud and that nobody would admit to needing help from a charity. I, however, convinced him that if I could get three to five stories, this would work.

I posted my initial request on our employee site, hoping for a few responses from the willing eyes. Within the first twenty-four hours, my inbox exploded with over a hundred passionate narratives about United Way. Some were benign, such as children attending a United Way funded daycare facility. Others were harder, like having to place a dying parent in a United Way funded hospice. And a few were heartbreaking, when an employee whose spouse had abused her physically, sexually, and emotionally and finally gathered the courage to leave her husband, but had no one to take her in since her abusive spouse had isolated her from her family and friends, a common tactic for abusers. She called 2-1-1, United Way's National Resource Hotline, and was directed to a shelter nearby. They also found her pro-bono legal services and an advocate to provide moral support at court as she faced her soon-to-be ex. I was in tears as I read the extreme details of her story.

Unbeknownst to me, this was the start of a successful run that eventually led to leaving my beloved UPS for United Way. Over the four campaigns I ran, the donation revenue grew from $48 million to $65 million. And in addition to United Way, we also supported numerous other non-profit organizations. In partnership with the Boys and Girls Clubs, we delivered driving classes for teenagers via our Road Code program, the safety training for UPS drivers. We brought the Road Code simulators to our booths at the various conferences we sponsored and had cutouts of the drivers and vehicles, allowing the attendees to become a UPSer for a minute. It was a great way for people to engage with a brand they loved and connect with "the truck" and its drivers. Our photographers uploaded the photos they took to participants' social media pages with a UPS branded frame and the partner whose conference it was, signifying our support of that community. Everyone had a blast! Having never had a marketer in the Foundation before, there were many opportunities for me to try out new ideas with the staff.

In addition to the United Way campaign, I also managed the Diversity investment portfolio and worked with the pre-eminent non-profits in that space: the National Urban League, Unidos U.S. (formerly National Council of La Raza), the Organization of Chinese Americans, and the Human Rights Campaign, among them. One of the organizations in my portfolio was the 100 Black Men of America.

I was the very "why" a white girl was given the diversity portfolio in my first meeting. At their annual meeting, I was one of four women in the room—and the only white person. It was yet another time in my life I'd been the only one of something, but this was somehow different. As I sat at my table of eight while they served lunch, I was acutely aware of my whiteness which was shining brightly in that room, and reflected upon what it must have been like to be the first, or the only, person of color to be somewhere: a classroom, a college lecture hall, a lunch counter. Unlike those "others" and "firsts," I wasn't met with resistance or hatred because of my skin color; I was warmly welcomed. For years, the "100" as they were known, joked about "the 100 black guys and our one white girl."

While CIP had exposed me to different demographics living in circumstances with which I was not familiar, the diversity organization gave me the opportunity to expand my awareness. Not being innately familiar with the challenges faced by the BIPOC (Black, Indigenous, People of Color) communities, being placed in that role exposed me to the challenge and impact agendas. I began to understand the systemic inequities that are endemic to our society, how policy agendas were set, and even the culture of how racial and ethnic groups we supported. More importantly, I would also be able to share everything I learned with others like me who were also unaware.

I was even awarded a seat on United Way's Global Corporate Leaders Advisory Council and eventually became the Council Chair. At the end of my term, the team composed of my counterparts from other corporations who supported United Way, gifted me a single red, white, and blue shoe with a super high heel. Its mate was kept at the organization and was passed to the incoming chair as their gavel—an entertaining tradition that continued for quite a while. That single magical shoe might have even been the source of my strength in my triumph over United Way's powerful forces I would soon come to encounter.

Chapter 12

"I have learned that as long as I hold fast to my beliefs and values – and follow my own moral compass – then the only expectations I need to live up to are my own."
Michelle Obama

United Way Worldwide
Alexandria, Virginia
Fall 2020
Approximately 7 p.m.

Given the alternative of going back to a boring hotel room and watching TV, it was common for me to work late hours at the office. This particular evening, however, would force me to lose sleep. As I finished up my own personal battles of the day, with zero unread emails in my inbox, one of my favorite employees knocked on my door....

I was surprised to see a face at my door so late and waved to Taylor that it was fine to come on in. The usually bubbly, young woman with the quick, bright smile was not the person I saw in front of me. At the time, she was the administrative assistant to one of the senior leaders on my team and was an intelligent, hardworking, and charismatic employee. She had expressed an interest in growing into a larger role and had even applied for a mid-level position that would place her on *Harasshole's* team.

Naively, I had initially not been concerned about her reporting to him because I thought the chances were slim that she would actually land the position. Professionally, however, she was not yet ready for the role, and there were multiple other candidates who were more qualified.

Taylor had obviously thought very hard about what she was going to say because as she nervously took her seat, she jumped right into telling me about her recent experience at a happy hour with a few members of the executive team.

Over the course of the next hour, Taylor confided with me about how uncomfortable *Harasshole* had made her feel. She divulged what had occurred, in what can best be described as *Harasshole* aggressively flirting with her.

It goes without saying, even after a long day of work, that my brain went into overdrive. I felt for her, she was young, attractive, and applying for a role under *Harasshole's* direct staff, she was an easy target.

I reassured her that it was a serious matter and one that she needed to discuss with HR or at least her direct supervisor. Even though the chances were slim, I was now concerned about the possibility of her joining his team.

Perhaps she too began to realize the seriousness of what she was describing to me, because she instantly employed a nervous humor defense mechanism and joked, "I can't help it if I'm all that!"

The following week, I reached out to both Taylor's manager and the HR team to ensure that both were aware of and investigating what had occurred. I was assured that it was being handled.

Now in retrospect, after all that has occurred, I partially blame myself. Had I ignored any signs? Had I been proactive enough in taking preventative measures or following up?

Perhaps I did not express how seriously concerned I was at the time. The one thing that I now know is that the biggest mistake in judgment I had made was in trusting that our HR department would do their job. It was not until well after I was fired that I learned that nothing had actually been done at all.

Chapter 13

"A strong woman looks a challenge dead in the eye and gives it a wink." Gina Carey

I LOVED my job at the Foundation. (Oh shit... there I go, I committed the cardinal sin by saying it out loud!)

In January 2015, I was unfortunately given a new assignment within the HR function and had to leave the Foundation and the job I loved so much.

In June, I received a surprising call from the Chief of Staff, at United Way. He knew I was no longer in the Foundation and yet still asked to set up a call with their CEO; he had indicated in confidence that this was not UPS-related. I had a great working relationship with the Chief of Staff and was curious about what they wanted to discuss.

As an aside, from this point forward, no names will be used for legal reasons, only titles, as there is still a pending legal case.

During the call, the CEO shared with me that they were looking for a new CMO and, before hiring a search firm, he wanted to check to see if I'd be interested. After all, I had already demonstrated how to lead a successful United Way campaign given the donation growth at the Foundation.

Were I to accept the position, I would be working at United Way Worldwide (UWW), the de facto headquarters for the global network, in Alexandria, Virginia, just outside of Washington, D.C. The responsibilities sounded exciting, and I'd be directly reporting to the CEO. I would oversee the marketing and communications teams while working to reframe United Way's brand, which after 135 years, needed to appeal to the next two generations of donors and volunteers. I loved brand work and communications.

This was certainly an unexpected turn of events, and I needed some time to think about the offer that was made during the call. Even though I didn't particularly love my new role at UPS, it wasn't so bad that I considered leaving, and I wasn't actively looking for a new job. And let's not forget what I said earlier, "If you didn't like your job at UPS, don't sweat it; you won't be there long."

The year before, I had gotten remarried. There was a prior marriage and starter husband, but none of that is relevant and it ended years ago. My new husband's job was in Atlanta and there was no place like home. My "platinum husband package" also included a gift with purchase, a stepdaughter. I told the CEO I was interested but needed to think about it and couldn't relocate. His response was, "Can you fly?" And with a grin, I replied, "No, but Delta can."

That evening, I shared with my other half the dream offer that the CEO proposed. He encouraged me to take it, telling me that, unlike my current job, when I spoke about helping make the world a better place through this new role, my face lit up. The UPSide (no pun intended!) was that I would still be closely collaborating with UPS and the Foundation, given the relationship between the two organizations. And so the decision was made that this new venture was my future.

After a series of interviews and negotiations, in August 2015, the night before we left on vacation to Turkey where we would spend five days on the Aegean Sea away from civilization, I accepted the position at United Way. I was sad to be leaving UPS, but I was excited to start an inspiring new dream career. I was confident I had made the right decision. Or had I...? That October, I formally resigned from UPS. The send-off was filled with sincere wishes as I ventured into my new post. Little did I know back then how badly I was going to need them.

The relaxing few weeks I took off before starting at United Way were short-lived, as not only did I have to travel almost every week to my office in Alexandria, but also across the United Way global network, which spanned nearly 1,800 communities, across more than forty countries and territories worldwide. Fortunately, the transition from UPS was not terribly challenging as I was able to build off my previous experience there; the United Way structure was very similar to the franchise model I had worked on with The UPS Store launch.

The adventure began on November 1, the eve of my first day at my new job, when I flew to Ronald Reagan Airport and took a cab from the airport to my new home three blocks from United Way headquarters, a Sheraton Hotel well past its prime. I was excited but nervous. I hadn't started a new job in fifteen years. I made sure to introduce myself to the hotel staff that was on duty that night as I'd be spending a lot of time there. One thing the Chief of Staff of United Way had once said about me when asked by a magazine doing a story on me was this: "Lisa's work is rooted in her compassion for others. When Lisa goes on location to shoot real stories about real people, she comes back with new friends... she does this not only on the job but everywhere she goes. She gets to know more about Lyft drivers during a five-mile trip than most people would in five years." What can I say? I'm a people person. Or at least I used to be.

I walked around three blocks in each direction to get a feel for my new neighborhood. Finding both Trader Joe's and Harris Teeter within that radius was a big score. There was a gym literally right next door to the office. I was set.

On that first Monday morning, bright and early, I arrived at the office ready to start my first weekly executive team meeting. The sun was shining bright, radiating off the Potomac as I entered the lobby with its two-story floor to ceiling wall of windows. I was ready. I entered the elevator of the five-story building, punching "5" for the floor to which I was headed for my first Executive Management Team (EMT) meeting. The culture shock set in immediately. UPS was formal, professional, business-like. People shook hands. As I approached the executive conference room, the COO, "Mr. Handsy" (for his propensity, as I would soon learn, to always touch women), came forward to greet me—with a hug—and a kiss on the cheek. Okay, that was weird. (Visualize the confused face emoji.) "Welcome. We're happy to have you here." My discomfort level was palpable.

The President of the U.S. division was the only other woman on the team besides me. The Chief Financial Officer, the Chief Strategy Officer, Chief of Staff, the International President, and the Chief Investor Relations Officer—all male. At any given point in my tenure there, women composed no more than thirty percent of the executive team. There was at any given point only one person of color on the team. Perhaps that in and of itself should have been a clue. In all of today's talk about diversity, while thirty percent may sound "good," there were three women to six men. The propensity for sports talk was overwhelming. The opportunity for shoe talk was non-existent.

The first couple of weeks were a bit of a blur. Before I even had the opportunity to see my office or meet my own team,

Chapter 13

I found myself in a meeting with many of the CEOs of local United Way offices.

Fortunately, I'm big on preparation and had requested and studied an organization chart prior to starting, so I at least had names and titles of my staff of about fifty people. When I was finally able to have my first team meeting, I wasted no time getting started by first sharing my leadership approach:

- The only real mistake is if someone dies. That's the only thing we can't fix. The rest are just learning experiences,
- Because my name is at the top of the org chart does not mean I have all the answers. If you have an idea or a thought, bring it up; we all have value to contribute,
- If my approach to or interactions with you don't work for you, please tell me. I'm likely unaware and doing it unintentionally, but I can't stop it if I don't know about it.

I had lunch every day with different people where I got to know them and United Way. I spent hours and days scouring through past work, reports, and documents to gain an in-depth knowledge of the organization. And before I knew it, it was Thanksgiving and the holiday season.

I started 2016 off running at a hundred miles an hour as I threw myself even deeper into my new role; there was plenty of work to be done to modernize and reframe the brand. I quickly understood that over ninety percent of United Way revenue was raised through the Baby Boomer and GenX members of the workplace, yet these demographics were aging out, being swiftly replaced by Millennials.

Research conducted prior to my arrival suggested that when asked, most people could only name one of the three areas United Way supported its communities: Health, Education, and Financial Stability. More importantly, the new generation's attitude was contrasting to how United Way operated. The non-profit was failing to catch on with the new expectations and inspiring the younger employees to donate. This next generation of donors didn't just want to give once a year when the annual United Way campaign occurred in their place of work; they wanted to do "evergreen giving"—all year, when and where they felt the need to do so. They also wanted a more engaged philanthropic experience; being able to see via webcam, for example, villagers in a developing country using a well they helped fund.

My understanding from the CEO was that I was to pick up the project from where my predecessor had left off and quickly bring it to a close. Yet no more than two months into the project, he blind-sided me with his comment that he hadn't liked my predecessor's work and was disappointed that I had decided to follow in her footsteps—I was shocked by his sudden change in perspective. Initially, I thought I might have misunderstood, but I'd soon come to realize that this was a normal pattern that I would have to learn how to navigate.

Equipped with that newly gained knowledge, the direction I later proposed was radically different than anything United Way had ever done before. It was this new brand direction that I was asked to present in the board meeting and later at our international conference of all the local United Ways in May 2016 in Vancouver, Canada.

Our research indicated two glaring problems: each local United Way worked in distinct ways, and their narrative was not consistent. While they all focused on education, in Des Moines, Iowa, it was about the third-grade reading

Chapter 13

level. However, in Milwaukee, Wisconsin, attention was on teen pregnancy in high school. And further abroad, in Mumbai, India, their local United Way worked to ensure that adolescent girls had access to clean restroom facilities. All were focused on education but with different goals and approaches. Internally as a brand, we had no consistency. And if we couldn't talk about ourselves the right way, neither could anyone outside of the organization.

The last major brand campaign United Way had launched was Live United, in 2008, and the following year, brand awareness, one of the key metrics tracked, hit its peak. The creative group designed Live United t-shirts showing people from various walks of life coming together. Black and white. Old and young. Gay and straight. However, the message wasn't clear on what United Way stood for or actually did, and the organization began suffering a gradual decline from that point forward. Not understanding what we did made it harder for people to trust—and if they didn't trust the organization, why would they trust us with their contributions? This was no different than a marketing challenge with any product. If people don't know what the product does, they're not going to buy it. Hey, I have a *whatchamacallit* on sale today for $100—want one?

The team was energized and ready to confront the challenge. Our "fight language" brought our three main focuses front and center in a transparent way, and only in fifteen words: United Way fights for the health, education, and financial stability of every person in every community.

I was proud of this radical new shift in brand positioning, but then again, I was also intimately acquainted with it—we had to see the reaction within the network.

The morning we debuted the campaign internally, I wondered if I'd still have a job after the meeting.

I positioned myself in the very center of the large conference room, which held about 1,500 people so that I could gauge the audience's reaction. The lights went down, and the short, two-and-a-half-minute video played. When the lights came back up, the room was eerily silent. "That's it," I thought to myself, "dead in the water—they hate it!" Then there was the sound of applause, quiet at first and building to a good solid crescendo.

During the coffee break, I was confronted with a variety of viewpoints from the local United Way CEOs: some loved the concept and praised me, some weren't sure, and some scowled at it. Clearly, we were not as United as I thought we were, which became ever clearer as I continued my tenure at the organization.

Chapter 14

"Doubt is a killer. You just have to know who you are and what you stand for."
Jennifer Lopez

Later that summer, we began testing the message for resonance and educating the organizations under the United Way umbrella on the new approach. We couldn't simply force them to adopt our new branding, and so to ensure a successful launch, we needed to conduct more research so that we could back our strategy up with more data. When exposed to the "fight language" and supporting visuals, people were inspired to join our fight and donate. And if they were already giving, they'd give more. The testing results clearly validated this new direction.

While our market research validated our new way forward, infusing this vision and language throughout every corner of the organization wasn't going to be a walk in the park. From our on-hold messages to email signatures, to how we framed our public policy agenda, our message had to be seamlessly woven throughout every single touchpoint at United Way.

With the challenge being clearly defined for us, we began creating the materials needed to roll this out: TV and radio spots to produce, print ads to create, brochures, brand guidelines, messaging architecture, annual reports, and so much more. By the time we were finished, the entire network would need to be convinced that this strategic shift was the way of the future.

And within a few months, we were ready to launch our first suite of public service announcements (PSAs) across the major television networks. It was during our first PSA shoot in Miami, Florida, in January 2017 where I had a life-changing moment that validated my wholehearted belief in why I left UPS for United Way.

It was only fifty-one degrees—cold for Miami—when we arrived in the Overton community for filming. We chose this not-so-great neighborhood for the aesthetic it offered the video, despite the fact it required the Miami police to accompany us for safety.

As I scoped out the area, I found a spot with a massive pile of trash—boxes, bags, newspapers—stacked along the fence we would use for our shot. I happened to glance down and saw a hand sticking out the form under the pile of trash. OH MY GOD!!! "There's a body under here," I thought in a panic. And then... the hand moved. THERE WAS A PERSON UNDER ALL THAT!

To make a long story short, Deon was homeless and was huddled under the pile of trash, trying to stay warm. Now one thing about me, as I've told you before, is that I will literally talk to a rock. If it talks back, that's even better. And with Deon, I didn't hesitate and immediately introduced myself to him and explained what we were doing there. He had heard of United Way. "You're the people that help people in need," he exclaimed. He knew that we were the organization who fought for every person in every community.

Deon had been on the streets "for a minute" as he shared with me. It hadn't been that long ago that he used to have a roof over his head, an apartment near the beach. A car.

Chapter 14

A job. Food on the table. Living life like the rest of us. Not a high roller but more than just scraping by. Then there was a car accident. Four people in the other car, three in Deon's car; Deon, his mother, and his aunt. Deon was the only person who walked away from the scene.

Psychological trauma, likely survivor's guilt coupled with mounting medical bills his insurance didn't cover, expedited his journey to the streets. Excessive absenteeism resulted in a job loss. He fell behind on his rent. The car got repossessed.

His story is hardly the first of its kind. The gap between getting by, surviving, and sliding towards the bottom in this country is razor thin. Sadly, the majority of the population is only four to six paychecks away from homelessness. In 2020, more than half of American adults had $5000 or less in savings. The median savings account held a balance of $3500, which makes it hard not to fall behind when faced with unexpected circumstances.

I knew in my heart that Deon and I had intersected for a reason. He WAS the very person for whom United Way fought—he was the face of whom we were fighting for. Thus I told the production team that I wanted Deon to be featured in the PSA. They pushed back; he's not 'talent.' But that was exactly WHY I wanted him. He was real. He was credible and authentic. His face, his haunting pain, his story became my raison d'être at United Way—even when things would become unbearable.

Deon became the face of the campaign. My hopes for him were twofold: that he would consider going to a shelter, and that someone—anyone—would see the spot and say, "That's my uncle, cousin, former co-worker, friend," and come forward to help. Sadly, none of that happened. Ever since that shoot, I kept a framed picture of Deon on my desk at work the entire time I was at United Way. He was my WHY: the *why* I left corporate America to take a job with no stock options; the *why* I lived away from home every week and often felt like an Airbnb guest in my own home on weekends; the *why* my job never felt like work.

The PSAs launched in April of 2017, and the wild, successful ride began. The first-year survey data indicated seventy percent of the United Way network had adopted the new brand. The following year, we reached over ninety percent. By May, I was such a known entity within so much of the network that at our annual conference in Orlando, Florida, the local United Way CEOs all wanted to take selfies with me. Although I was uncomfortable with selfies, I knew this was a cultural thing for United Way, and I was flattered by their consideration.

The successful rebranding campaign paved the way for many amazing experiences with United Way. I got to attend the Superbowl every year through our relationship with the NFL, rang the closing bell at NASDAQ, and spoke at a variety of events. I loved my job, not just because of the benefits it brought—don't get me wrong, I did enjoy them—but because of what I was actually able to achieve. I was part of a team that was able to make a difference in a person's life somewhere in the world, even without meeting her or him face-to-face. Somebody, somewhere whom we'd never met would have a better tomorrow because of what we did yesterday, and that was immensely satisfying and gratifying. This role represented the perfect fusion of my parents in me: my mom's non-profit work at March of Dimes with my dad's creative side as an advertiser and marketer.

Furthermore, I was able to capitalize on my love of travel and culture. I went to China in the fall of 2017 to visit with the China Charity Federation, one of our non-profit partners. Together, we ran a program that provided support and care for children whose parents had migrated to urban areas in order to make a living and couldn't bring along children either because of limited employer-provided housing or the inability to register for a school outside of the province in which they were born. Not many were lucky enough to have a relative or friend who could help, which thus resulted in social development and emotional issues from not having parents or family present in addition to educational challenges.

At the end of each day, I journaled, sharing my scribbles with my team in the U.S., hoping to bring them along the journey with me as I described the work we did, the people we met, the environment we were in, and how much rice I'd eaten that day! I don't even really care for Chinese food here in the U.S. other than pot stickers and egg rolls; over there was a whole other story.

As I sat in a classroom with young Chinese girls busy with their artwork, I recalled my parents displaying my treasured artwork and drawings on the refrigerator door. It hit me that these girls had no parents at home, nobody to complement their creations, perhaps even no fridge door to hang them on.

My translator explained to the girls that we put the children's artwork around the house for the entire family to enjoy. I asked if I could take their artwork home for the United Way family to display in our office kitchen. That artwork traveled nearly twelve thousand miles back to Alexandria, guarded as one of my most precious possessions. I displayed the artwork gratefully on the break room fridge with a note explaining the story behind it, along with the pictures of the girls.

Most of the work we did happened in the shadows. Sometimes, especially after a rough day at the office, the work we did in the field seemed so distant since we weren't directly involved with the recipients, unlike a local United Way. By putting faces to the those whom we served, whether through the artwork, and my attempt at journaling the details of the trip and sharing out near real-time, this was my way of trying to help my team really see and feel that our efforts affected change in the world, and the work we did truly mattered to someone in need. Just like Deon.

Chapter 15

> "Whenever you see a successful woman, look out for three men who are going out of their way to try to block her."
> Yulia Tymoshenko

United Way was not UPS. I would routinely and unreservedly shout out loud to myself and anyone else who would listen, "I LOVE MY JOB!!!" Every day was invigorating and filled with gratification.

However, despite the love I had for my job and the initial success I experienced with the new strategy, it was clear that United Way's business model was under duress. Yes, it was the first non-profit to conduct annual workplace campaigns, with roughly sixty thousand companies supporting the cause. And yes, giving contributions was second nature for the Baby Boomers and GenXers who had grown up with these annual campaigns. But as the demographics of the employees began shifting rapidly with Millennials entering the workplace, charitable contributions collected during annual United Way campaigns commenced a steady decline.

It wasn't because the next generation of donors did not want to contribute; they simply had a different approach to charity. Undoubtedly, these younger employees wanted to give and support charitable causes, yet the framework offered by their employer—and by United Way—did not provide a channel that was culturally and technologically relevant to them. This generation did not want to be told whom they should give to and when they should do it, but rather embraced the concept of "evergreen giving," meaning they would contribute when they wanted, and to an organization that mattered to them at that particular point in time.

Imagine a cold New York City morning. You get off the subway to go to your office in a high-rise building in the Financial District. (This is, of course, a pre-Covid world when we actually used to go to the office.) Walking to your office building, you approach Starbucks, desperately needing a $7 Venti Latte with a soymilk upcharge of 50¢ to jumpstart your morning. As you leave Starbucks, enjoying the smell of your freshly brewed cup of coffee, you encounter a homeless person on the street. You are suddenly very aware of the delicious, expensive warm coffee in your hand. You want to help this person whom life didn't treat kindly. In the old business model, you'd make a *note to self*: "United Way campaign is in six months, remember to donate to a homeless shelter." Under our newly proposed technology-driven model, you would be able to use your smartphone on the spot to either donate *or* find somewhere to volunteer. Higher relevancy; which allowed us to capitalize on the emotion and desire of that moment and convert it to action.

Just as this exciting new endeavor was starting to take shape, the Chief Strategy Officer (CSO) leading this critical project resigned, which gave United Way the opportunity to expand the role of this position and create the new title of Chief Strategy and Transformation Officer. The person leading the digital transformation of United Way would immediately be tasked with launching the new technology platform. Soon after the position was announced, we

Chapter 15

received a candidate recommendation from the a local United Way CEO, a member of her own staff.

In October 2017, I was asked by our CEO to interview the new candidate since he would be part of the executive management team. The morning the candidate arrived, my assistant escorted him up from the lobby. I stepped into the hallway to greet him. Let's set the scene here: remember, I'm five feet tall, five-five in heels; he, however, was about six foot two. As I extended my hand and said, "Hi, I'm Lisa Bowman," he stepped very close to me, directly into my personal space, and looked down at me. In our first verbal interaction, he said smugly, "You're really intimidating," adding, "I hear you have a reputation for getting shit done and taking no shit."

His provocative, somewhat aggressive introduction, stunned me, but in an extra effort to remain professional, I replied, "I'm only five feet tall. How intimidating could I possibly be?" Honestly, even if I were in my ruby slippers, I don't see myself as an intimidating person!

We moved into my office, where we started the interview and discussed what his role would be in the new position. His odd introduction was just the beginning as the conversation continued to turn even more bizarre. He proceeded to swear throughout the interview, even more, he also warned me that the two of us would "tangle" and that he was "manic." I replied that if, in fact, we "tangled," we'd resolve it professionally behind closed doors. His response was, "That would be fun."

I was shaken by his unexpected behavior. His inappropriate manners were like nothing I had ever experienced at a workplace before, especially from a person who was INTERVIEWING FOR A JOB—an executive role, please keep in mind! I completed the interview as professionally as possible and escorted him to the CFO's office, where he would continue the process. The CFO later shared with me that the candidate had also conducted himself awkwardly with him during the interview; not only did he avoid making eye contact, but he spent the entire interview writing emails on his laptop instead of engaging with the CFO. Maybe it's just me, but I'm guessing if you've had experience managing and interviewing people, you, too, would find this odd, right?

When my boss, the CEO, called me for feedback about the candidate, I was conflicted about what to say. I told him that given his background and experience, the candidate appeared to be technically competent for the role, but he was "socially awkward," as I politely put it, and that I was reluctant to fully endorse hiring him as a part of the executive team. As I shared the comments the candidate made, specifically the one about my intimidating reputation, the CEO replied, "But Lisa, you are intimidating." Seriously? I never thought of myself as intimidating. At all.

What did this mean? Two men had just told me I was intimidating.

Chapter 16

"No one can make you feel inferior without your consent."
Eleanor Roosevelt

As any good marketer would, I set off to investigate whether this perception of me was an emerging trend that I should be aware of. Were there many others who felt this way? If they were intimidated by me, was this my problem, or theirs? An insecure male who was threatened by a female?

It should come as no surprise to anyone that intimidation plays a significant role in our daily social interactions. Some appear physically intimidating, while others come across as imposing because of their personality, intellect, wealth, or social status. Whatever the origin, we rarely discuss it openly and freely. Hence, those who intimidate us often have no idea how we perceive them or their behavior. Just like any other threat, when you internalize or conceal your emotions, there can be real risks. Intimidation behaves like a perceived threat (because it actually IS to the person who is intimidated) and can easily trigger what's known as a "fight or flight" response; an instinctive physiological response to a threatening situation, which readies you to either resist violently or to run away.

On the other hand, for those who experience intimidation, it typically boils down to the feeling that the person you're interacting with is more powerful than you.

Even the most seemingly secure individuals are intimidated sometimes, though not always by whom you'd expect.

First, in this case, the candidate was, in theory, a successful businessman and had the technical skills and the know-how for the job. Further, he interviewed as my peer, not as my subordinate. Second, the CEO was my boss. I wasn't more powerful than either of them. So what did this all mean?

A 2013 study conducted by *Psychology Today* will help clarify. It found that people were judged as more intimidating when they tilted their faces slightly, either upward or downward. I was five foot five in my heels; the candidate was six foot two. Did the fact that I had to tilt my face slightly upward to make eye contact create a sense of intimidation? I almost always have to do that.

Moreover, a sustained, direct gaze tends to elicit strong fight-or-flight reactions. Yes, of course, I held a direct gaze—eye contact is important when you meet someone, no?

In the end, our most substantial feelings of intimidation often correspond to our own insecurities. Although I wasn't looking to spend my time psychoanalyzing either the candidate's or the CEO's issue with self-esteem, it's interesting to consider the idea.

For reasons unknown to me, the CEO disregarded feedback from the CFO and me. I have no indication of what the other executive team members who interviewed him shared with our boss, and we never interviewed any other candidates for the role.

Almost immediately, the candidate was hired and eventually became known to me as my "Harasshole."

Chapter 17

"You may not control all the events that happen to you, but you can decide not to be reduced by them."
Maya Angelou

Lisa's home office
Atlanta, Georgia
Tuesday, May 11, 2021

"Ms. Bowman, are you okay? Do you need to break for a few minutes?" asked the Equal Employment Opportunity Commission (EEOC) investigator assigned to my case.

"No, I'm fine, thank you, let's continue," I lied in response as I quickly searched to switch off the camera on Microsoft Teams so no one in the virtual meeting could see me crying.

Shortly after my initial EEOC filing, COVID-19 rocked the world. The pandemic caused processing delays within just about every government agency across the country, and the EEOC was no exception. The United States Equal Employment Opportunity Commission, or EEOC for short, is the government agency responsible for "enforcing federal laws that make it illegal to discriminate against a job applicant or an employee because of the person's race, color, religion, sex, sexual orientation, national origin, age, disability along with a number of other criteria. For my case against United Way, a ruling in my favor for harassment or retaliation would be the sledgehammer I needed to send a message that they would finally hear—a message they could not continue to ignore, and one that hopefully would foster change for others in the future.

My attorney told me the process could take a while, but as weeks turned into nine months, I decided to take matters into my own hands. I contacted and emailed anyone within the department whom I could get reach. Finally, after what felt like an eternity of waiting, I finally got someone on the phone, who in turn put me in contact with the lead investigator for my case. Eventually, I received a simple email from them asking for an appointment in two weeks. I was elated!

Ever the organized, and diligent student, I followed up with a note to confirm and ask if there was anything I could provide to him to help the process, or if I could prepare in any way prior to our meeting. I didn't let "no" for an answer influence my next steps, and so I spent a week reviewing notes and preparing documents. One benefit of living in this current COVID world was the advent of virtual, online meetings. Rather than being a nervous wreck, sitting in person across from the investigator, drinking stale coffee and stuck in a dated, wood-paneled, pop-corn ceiling conference room, speaking into a tape recorder (at least that's how I imagined it), now I could be in my comfort zone. Sitting in my own home office, dressed professionally, at least from the waist up, with index cards of talking points at my disposal.

My attorney called me the day before to walk me through the process, review a few critical items with me, and more importantly, assure me that it would go well. I spent most of the night before awake, deep inside my head. I was confident in what I was going to say. Nothing but the facts—truthful and direct. But still, I was nervous. Up to this point,

Chapter 17

due to Covid's social distancing restrictions, I hadn't even seen my lawyer's face!

Yet now, as I finally managed to turn off my laptop's camera, I realized how raw this entire experience still was for me. The investigator was kind and asked basic questions simply to verify the facts, but for me, just recounting the events brought all the emotions flooding back.

I felt a sense of relief and pride as the call wrapped up with a few legal, procedural statements. I was anxious to hear about the next steps we would be taking, though little did I know that I would be forced to wait patiently for two years.

Chapter 18

"It's not your job to like me, it's mine."
Byron Katie

Harasshole officially joined our team in January 2018. From day one, his poor attitude and behavior that was demonstrated during the initial interview continued. He was antagonistic and would routinely make nasty comments towards me, which would then be followed by a compliment. And while they may have started off with business subjects as his target, over time, the abuse deteriorated to verbal, personal attacks. Though not every comment may have been considered explicitly transgressive, the supposedly minor, peculiar remarks, such as addressing me as Bowman, Boss, or Boss Lady, quickly became apparent they were here to stay; that is, unless I took matters into my own hands.

How does one handle such nuanced, carefully honed slights? I certainly didn't arrive at United Way with a user manual on how to deal with such unwanted name calling and was thus headed into uncharted territory. I decided to treat him in a similar manner and began addressing him as "LAST NAME." He didn't find that amusing and, in retaliation, completely stopped using any sort of salutation when interacting with me.

Little did I know this was just a preview of how I would spend the rest of my career at United Way.

Each day came with a different set of challenges. Just as the use of "Boss Lady" subsided, *Harasshole* started to engage in a regular pattern of challenging behavior towards me, which included the scheduling of weekly one-on-one meetings, then not showing up or rescheduling them at the last minute. One could excuse such actions if there were just a modicum of mutual communication, yet he rarely responded to my emails, if at all. Case in point: on one occasion, he had scheduled a meeting in Toronto, Canada, with our technology partners and requested that I attend. He then failed to respond to my multiple follow-ups regarding the meeting details until the week prior, subsequently telling me I could join by phone (for two FULL DAYS of meetings) when all of the other parties involved were meeting in person. To further compound the issue, he did not even provide the dial-in information to allow me access into the meeting. And even worse, during the Toronto meeting, he established communications protocols with the local United Way offices that would cut my team entirely out of the conversation and process.

Looking at all of his actions in aggregate, one could interpret his conduct like a series of deliberate attempts to provoke me into confrontation. And again, I ask myself, *why?* What drives such behavior in someone? Never in my entire career had someone behaved this way towards me; it was hurtful and beyond unprofessional. I had no idea what I had done to be the recipient of this; I kept thinking and hoping things would change for the better—but it never did.

On another occasion, I was asked to join him in Miami, Florida, for a meeting on June 11, 2018. When I requested to review the meeting agenda and inquired about what

Chapter 18

he envisioned my role would be during the meeting, he curtly told me to "sit there and just hang out." I clearly understood that his intention was to secure the participating organizations as internal customers for the technology platform being developed for the network, and so I mentioned that I had a good working rapport with the three local United Way organizations who would be in attendance and that my established relationships with them could add credibility to his pitch and support the overall project goals.

Harasshole offered to complete the first draft of the presentation. And though I should have known not to trust him by this point, I nonetheless left it with him. (I almost always inherently see the good in people. I know—my bad!) After asking for the presentation deck multiple times to review before the meeting, he failed to share the slides with me until nearly 10 p.m. the evening before the pitch.

As if it couldn't get any worse, on the day of the presentation, four slides into the presentation, *Harasshole* stated to the group, "I was going to let Lisa present some of this, but she's probably not capable." The attendees didn't know how to take such bizarre comments and so let out a burst of nervous laughter in reaction to it.

Where did that come from? I firmly stood up and responded, "You know what, I think I'll take the next chunk of this," and proceeded with the presentation until deciding to turn it back over to him so that he could present the slides that were specifically his.

When the meeting ended, the two of us remained in the conference room so that we each could wrap up on our own before departing.

While in there, my phone rang—it was my doctor's office. The week before the meeting, I had had my annual routine mammogram. Given that I was high-risk, as both my mother and my maternal aunt had passed from breast cancer at fifty and fifty-nine, respectively, I was diligent about surveillance. Still feeling at the prime of my youthful life, I'd already outlived my mom. I contemplated all the things she wanted to do (and I with her) that we never had the opportunity to accomplish as this cruel disease took her from us much too early.

When the doctor calls, it's typically with an "all clear" message following my mammogram visit. This time, given that I was sitting across from *Harasshole* in the conference room, I nearly let it go to voicemail. But for some reason, I felt compelled to hit the green button.

Without thinking, I answered the phone and asked the nurse practitioner to hold on for a minute. My stomach was turning with apprehension. There was no other place to take the call privately besides the conference room. Turning to *Harasshole*, I politely asked, "Could you please give me a minute alone here? This is my doctor's office, and I need some privacy to take the call."

He just stared at me blankly and remained where he was without saying a single word. I was fuming with rage and despised sharing the conference room with him. My anger subsided quickly as I listened to the nurse. Unfortunately, my mammogram indicated an irregularity. I turned my back for some privacy and spoke quietly to make the arrangements for a follow up visit. The news shook me; plus, there couldn't have been a worse time to try to set up a follow up visit.

I decided to schedule the biopsy procedure for Thursday, June 14. When I hung up with the doctor's office, my hands were shaking. Without skipping a beat and devoid of compassion, *Harasshole* said, "Sounds like you've got some issues." He continued to probe for a while, receiving no

Chapter 18

response from me. He actually had the guts to not only eavesdrop on my call but blatantly admit it! Who does that?

Admittedly, at that moment, I felt a deep desire to talk to someone for a bit of comfort and reassurance, but that someone certainly was not him. We weren't friends. We weren't even "colleagues" other than the simple fact that we had to collaborate on the same project. WHY on earth would he think I would willingly engage in conversation about something so personal to me?

The experience left me feeling vulnerable and violated, and I wished I could just fly as far away from him as I possibly could. Thankfully, I was able to wrap up the remainder of my work in record time. I stuffed my papers and belongings into my Louis Neverfull and got the hell out, with my stomach twisting and turning. Staving off a headache, I bolted for the airport. It wasn't until I got into the cab that I realized I was hyperventilating. During the drive to the airport, blankly staring out the window at the streets of Miami, with their colorful graffiti and Latin vibe infusing the air, my pulse began to even out.

At first, I thought the news had sent me spiraling back into an emotional tailspin about my mother. But then I realized it wasn't the call that stressed me out and left me breathless. I wasn't freaked out about the upcoming biopsy. To be honest, I had actually half expected it and was somewhat prepared for it. My mom was a warrior but had lost her battle with breast cancer at age fifty. I felt I was predestined for that diagnosis at some point, probably not too far out in the future. Remember, I come prepared, and I always have a plan. And if I were to receive a positive diagnosis, there would be a preemptive mastectomy, and possibly even a new and improved set of boobs—there is always an upside. I am not trying to be callous, or dismissive of the seriousness of any type of cancer, breast or other, or the pain endured from losing a loved one to this ruthless illness. The wounds of losing my mom still hurt. This was simply how I coped with my reality.

If it was not a medical scare, then what was it? What was the sudden stressor that left me feeling uneasy? Could *Harasshole* really be affecting me this much?

This experience made me realize that my interactions with *Harasshole* were starting to trigger some kind of physical-emotional response in me that I didn't like. I found myself tensing up when he was in proximity, dreading to be in meetings with him. But I couldn't complain about something like this, could I? Was he inappropriate? Definitely. Socially awkward? Certainly. But if I brought it up, how would that reflect on me? And, what would happen if I raised it? Who should I even raise it to? Would he escalate his behavior towards me, and would things worsen if he did actually get reprimanded? I felt like I was back in grade school, considering if I should snitch on the classroom bully to my teacher.

Later that week, during a conversation with our Chief of Staff, who always had a keen sense of right or wrong, I shared the exchange *Harasshole,* and I had in that Miami conference room. After hearing my story, he concurred that *Harasshole's* behavior was consistently "odd," and he "often misbehaved." It was a relief that at least others had witnessed it, and it wasn't all in my head. This is something I have learned by speaking with other women who have been in my situation. We constantly doubt ourselves and do not trust ourselves. We give too much benefit of the doubt to the harassers.

At the workplace, we learn to get along in a professional environment even if we don't mesh well together. This was a different game than I'd ever played before, and I didn't know the rules or even understand the desired outcome. What did a "win" look like for either of us? As uncomfortable as he made me, I just wanted to collaborate productively together in pursuit of our shared business goals.

Chapter 19

"She was powerful not because she wasn't scared but because she went on so strongly, despite the fear."
Atticus

Two days after my second breast biopsy, my heavily bandaged boob and I headed off to Brussels for a Global Board Meeting. This was my first visit to Brussels, so I blocked time in my schedule on Sunday afternoon to crisscross the historical landmarks. The tranquil vibe of the city was eerily different from the animosity that had built in the office in the past few months.

    I live my life in discovery mode and always welcome a good adventure. After the past week's stress, wandering in the square, gazing at the unique architecture of elegant guild houses surrounding the Grand-Place rejuvenated me. I hunted for the best waffles and dark chocolate in town; after all, a trip to Brussels is incomplete without having a belly filled with Belgian waffles with the creamiest ice cream! I slipped in, of course, some street shopping, a great little corner wine bar (Etiquette, if you happen to visit Brussels), and just soaked up the ambiance of the city as I enjoyed escaping from the ugly reality of my workplace. *Harasshole* didn't stay at the hotel with the rest of us, which provided a welcome reprieve from him.

    I found out that we had assigned seating for our Monday evening board dinner. I prayed to God, Allah, Buddha,

Mohammed, the Hindu deities, and even KimYe not to seat me anywhere near *Harasshole*. I'm not sure which one heard and answered my prayers, but I am grateful and thank you all!

Following the conclusion of the board meeting, I left Brussels and headed directly to Orlando for my next set of meetings which began at 8:30 a.m. the next morning. During my presentation, the doctor's office called again; the message they left was that my test results were "inconclusive," and another biopsy was required. Regardless of the fact that I was alone to receive this news, away from home, and had just come back from the other side of the world, I wasn't shaken by this. It was a process, and I needed the follow it. I scheduled the second biopsy for July 3, a day before Atlanta's celebrated 10K Peachtree Road Race. As will probably come as no surprise to you by now, I lead my life on full throttle and had been a dedicated participant of the race for many years; I foolishly assumed I'd be fit to run six-plus miles the day after the biopsy. I was dead WRONG!

During the entire two-plus-hour procedure, I was face down on a table with holes in it where my breasts snuggly fit. The surgeon was underneath me on a dolly, guided by an MRI as she worked her magic. I felt like a car during an oil change! I was bruised and sore from the procedure—I was definitely not running, or even jogging, to the finish line.

Chapter 20

"It's possible to climb to the top without stomping on other people."
Taylor Swift

My stress level began to peak as the executive team's annual mid-year retreat, typically held around the Fourth of July, approached. Traditionally, the two-day meeting was off-site at a bed and breakfast venue about an hour away from the office. It was on a little island, Kent Island. The CEO loved it—the rest of us hated it, yet, no one had ever gathered enough courage to tell him the truth. We smiled and nodded as he mentioned how charming the place was. To be perfectly fair to the venue, even though it was not my style, as it was old and smelled musty with the kind of furnishings that made me itch, it had a welcoming, homey atmosphere. Unfortunately, our time there together as a team never felt welcoming or cozy.

While we were supposed to be bonding as an executive team during these retreats, they always failed miserably. This is how the evenings usually played out: following dinner, we'd head across the boggy yard to sit on the dock and fight off the mosquitoes that were hell-bent on taking full advantage of the All You Can Eat Executive Buffet. The guys would retreat to one end of the dock with cigars and talk business, while the women would be left to their own devices to talk "girl stuff," I suppose.

At every single retreat, the CEO's personality would rear its ugly head. There was always a loud blow-up at some point between the boss and a random team member, which would crush any bit of team-building spirit to the ground. We had a running joke about who this year's scapegoat would be, stopping just short of a betting pool on who the top three most likely victims of the retreat would be.

One year, the Chief Strategy Officer was ground zero with the CEO. We were in a conference room that looked like a dining room. The tension in the room was heavy; an old pedestal stand fan valiantly tried its best to move the thick air as it rotated back and forth, clicking at each turn. The hot and humid weather already made the environment uncomfortable even before the full-out clash between these two grown businessmen, unnecessarily leaving us all staring down at the table or excusing ourselves for yet another extended trip to the restroom.

Dealing with him when he unleashed his inner beast was a delicate art. He was a big man, neither warm nor friendly as you may perhaps expect a CEO of a charitable organization to be. He was often aggressive and combative. I wondered if he was also like this with his all-female family at home or if he was just playing a power game at the office where he held the cards and had the leverage.

The CEO had been at the top of the echelon for nearly twenty years. He was a life-timer who had spent his entire career at United Way, having been hired right out of college as a management trainee and then climbing the ladder throughout his tenure. I often used to find myself trying to find a reason to justify his behavior and look for context or an excuse, and my understanding was that the route of his behavior originated from a challenging background that was perhaps abusive and financially unstable. One thing about this man was that he always had to feel like the smartest guy in the room who had all the answers. He liked to remind people that he was the CEO. Sadly, I think back to all the encounters I witnessed and do not believe he has a thread of decency, regardless of what the cause was or not. After all, he was the one who had the sole power to stop *Harasshole's* behavior, yet he refused to wield it. Learning to navigate this minefield was a fine art, and I had learned that sometimes it was easier just to make him think my ideas were HIS.

In April of 2016, six months into my role, I had the luxury of personally experiencing one of his core character flaws: lack of empathy. I was in Chicago at the NFL draft for a new program launch. The night before, at dinner, my wallet was stolen out of my purse, which I had hung on the back of my chair. (Yes, ladies, we all know better, it's a bad habit of mine.)

The theft left me with no cash or credit cards far from home. I didn't even have an ID to board my flight home. (To make matters worse, I had a HUGE event the following day—nope, not stressed out at all! I'm being sarcastic in case you have not caught onto my humor this far into the book!)

My boss simply didn't care, did not even offer me cash for a meal or ensure I was okay with getting a ride to the airport. He. Simply. Did. Not. Care.

What he did care about were the photo ops and getting visibility with the Chicago Bears players. Now, I know I'm a big girl, but think for just a minute about how almost anyone else with an ounce of humanity would have reacted. I couldn't even take an Uber to the airport because I had to cancel my credit cards. I suppose I had expected some iota of empathy for what had happened on the most basic, human level.

Graciously, one of my team members used her ATM card to loan some cash to me, even though she was short on funds. Thank God, I am a freak who actually still carries a checkbook at the bottom of my purse and was able to write her a check on the spot.

The adventure behind getting through TSA at a major airport with no ID is a whole other thing, but let me just inform you, it can be done and involves the security suspiciously scrutinizing EVERY single item in your suitcase in detail. And I mean EACH AND EVERY one. I made it back to Atlanta without much more trouble, but the point of this story is to illustrate the type of person my boss actually was and my coming to terms with just who the CEO was. In retrospect, it's the biggest irony as he had such a black soul yet was the leader of the world's largest health and human services charity.

He had a wife and two daughters whom he revered, but I never felt like he had much respect for me or the other women in the workplace. When he went mano-a-mano with the guys, it was trench warfare; male egos clashing to find the Alpha. I honestly think he took it on as a sport. However, when it happened with the women, we were often accused of being emotionally invested in the topic at hand. I never felt like I or my female colleagues were on equal footing with the guys.

Throughout all of these encounters, I realized and came to accept who he was as a person. I lowered my expectations for any sort of positive relationship with him. And to be clear, my efforts kept the professional relationship still manageable until *Harasshole* appeared on the scene in early 2018.

Chapter 21

"Those that weather the storm are the great ones."
DJ Khaled

The culture of a company or office is often set by the boss, whom other members of the team see as the leader, and this certainly proved true here. What perhaps made it more challenging to discern in our environment is the fact that many of us worked from various locations outside the office. While I was at the United Way office most weeks, we all traveled extensively. Two or three of us were almost always on the road; therefore, as an executive team, we didn't spend much time together in the office. We met regularly as a team via weekly calls and one-on-one and just got our work done. (I think we all understand how easy and seamless that is to do now after a global shutdown.) However, during our annual retreats, the true colors presented themselves in all their glory.

In July 2018, we had our mid-year retreat. Unlike the previous gatherings, where the retreat was on an island, this year it was a bed and breakfast type venue in Alexandria, closer to the office. We had a third-party facilitator joining us who was a friend of the Chief Revenue Officer. I think we were all breathing at least a minimal sigh of relief that we wouldn't be playing "Non-profit Survivor" on the island this year.

We arrived at the new venue in the morning. The heavenly smell of freshly brewed coffee was welcome and tasted even more delicious. Serve me bad coffee, and we're done for the day, LOL. A good cup of coffee is one of the few vices I have besides dark chocolate and shoes. Alcohol isn't really my thing, and I don't smoke. In college, I had a roommate my sophomore year who was teeny tiny and smoked two packs of Marlboro Reds daily. I tried to join in, but my tobacco experiment was short-lived. I hated the taste, the way my hair and clothes smelled. Cigarette smoke and my sinuses did not get along. Two seconds of exposure to it, and I'm stuffed up. In the end, I had to move out.

The retreat was scheduled to last two days, which felt like an eternity at the outset. The first morning passed without incident, and I was glad that one hadn't happened—yet. But nevertheless, we continued to walk on eggshells, expecting to fall prey to the inevitable hazard that could befall us at any moment. It did come, but what we didn't expect was that the source would be different this year.

We started the afternoon with a breakout session in order to address a specific strategic task. I had clearly neglected my prayers to the Gods this time and ended up in the same group with *Harasshole*. Statistically, when eight people are broken into two small teams, chances were pretty high that I'd end up with him; I should have prioritized my prayers.

Growing up in the UPS culture, I had a habit of arriving early to meetings. ALWAYS. Late was a cardinal sin at *Brown*. If you were early, you were on time. If you were on time, you were late. And if you were late, you probably shouldn't attend. In my opinion, being late, or even trying to slip in at the exact starting time, was a sign of disrespect and lack of courtesy to your fellow colleagues.

Chapter 21

I was routinely teased at United Way for almost always being the first to arrive in the meeting room—especially for our executive team meetings. On the contrary, for *Harasshole*, being late was standard practice. It felt like a deliberate act to make an entrance and display that he was so busy that he couldn't be on time. To me, it was just a blatant show of disrespect for his colleagues and boss.

Back in the breakout session, I noticed how we had both purposefully sat as far away from each other as possible. The third-party facilitator was working with the four of us: myself, *Harasshole*, the Chief of Staff, and the Chief Revenue Officer. I let my guard down since the CEO was in the other group, and I thought I was in a safe harbor away from any potential outbursts during the breakout session. This time, however, instead of the CEO, Hurricane *Harasshole* blew into Alexandria that afternoon, unleashing 85 MPH winds and leaving a six-foot-two storm surge of crap in his wake.

It wasn't more than ten minutes into the breakout session that suddenly *Harasshole* stood up out of his chair. In that brief moment, I could instantly see the dark clouds swirling in his eyes, and I knew in that instant I couldn't stop what was coming, so I braced for impact.

Next, in great melodramatic fashion, he threw every item in front of him off the table, screaming, and yelled, "This just isn't working for me! I'm going to call my coach," and he raced out of the room.

Chills ran down my spine as I watched him in slow motion. I sat there frozen. We were all shell-shocked by his unbalanced, erratic behavior. The facilitator caught my eye and subtly arched her eyebrow as if to say, "What the hell was THAT?" I shook my head in disbelief and gave a tiny shrug.

Who knew what this was about? We were in the middle of a brainstorming exercise about general business strategies. Nothing about his or my work was mentioned. No criticism at all. We were discussing ideas for the upcoming fiscal year.

My two other colleagues were as perplexed as I was and chatted about what might have caused such a scene. We never reached an answer. It would remain one of those mysteries of the universe. We resumed where we left off, and *Harasshole* never rejoined us. Unfortunately, we weren't able to complete the full assignment as he had completely disrupted our flow and our thought process.

About thirty minutes after his outburst, the breakout groups returned to the meeting room where we began sharing the salient points of our discussions. *Harasshole* was still MIA.

Fortunately, the other team went first, but when it was our turn, the Chief of Staff told the CEO that we couldn't complete the assignment after *Harasshole's* disruption. I was thankful I wasn't the one who had to break this news. The CEO glanced at the facilitator, questioning the validity of what he was hearing. She gave a slight nod corroborating the event, and I felt like a seven-year-old first grader telling her teacher that the dog had eaten her homework.

When I walked out of the meeting room for fresh air during a break, I found *Harasshole* outside on the stairs, where he was ranting and raving on his phone. I could see him gesturing wildly with his hands and could hear his loud voice but couldn't make out what he was saying. His face was dark and sullen, a look I'd come to recognize when he didn't like the situation he was in. I learned to gauge his future state by that dark look.

The CEO and Chief Culture Officer came out of the session and spoke with him outside the building for a while. The CEO also spoke directly to the facilitator. This mandatory unscheduled break was awkward at best, and so we made the best of our time by checking our emails and making small talk in an attempt to avoid the uncomfortable subject at hand.

We reconvened about an hour later—all of us—at the table in the small conference room. The weirdness of the situation hung in the air like a low thick toxic fog. Neither the CEO nor the Chief Culture Officer (who was also responsible for all HR matters) addressed or acknowledged the situation with the group at large. It was as if it never happened.

The following day, several others from the office joined us in our meetings. For the remainder of the retreat, the tone and language that *Harasshole* took with us was base and vulgar. He didn't hesitate to use the "f-word" repeatedly in front of other executive team members (including his boss), mid-level management staff (including his direct reports), and even an external vendor. And it didn't stop there with the profanity, as he graced us all with a variety of other delightful words. What was most disheartening was that even though the CEO and Chief Culture Officer witnessed this unacceptable behavior firsthand, they never reprimanded or called him out about the choice of language he was using with his peers and subordinates.

Leaders should lead by example. To my disappointment, but not surprisingly, my boss failed at it that day. Even if *Harasshole's* actions were addressed with him in private, there was no apology from him, no talk of it at all.

While we failed to accomplish several of the strategic objectives of the retreat, I personally had a key take-away. It was the realization of the culture in which I was working and should have been the dawning of my understanding of how that would impact the events that would soon transpire. The fact that *Harasshole* was *allowed* to behave like that just a). gave him validation that it was okay—even accepted, and b). showed me that the CEO had a real problem with double standards and accountability—at least where *Harasshole* was concerned.

Chapter 22

"A woman with a voice is, by definition, a strong woman."
Melinda Gates

As summer wore on, the fall foliage around D.C. started to reveal its colors, turning a beautiful array of deep reds and oranges, a sign that winter and short, dark days were also around the corner. And like the days that grew shorter, so too did *Harasshole's* emails. By now, *Harasshole* would only respond to my emails with "sure" or "sure thing" and never actually address or respond to the contents of the emails. By that point, I had already lost any remote possibility of trusting him, nor did I want to be in his presence even for a second. I tried as hard as possible to communicate what I needed in writing in a clear and simplistic tone so that nothing could be left open for interpretation.

In those moments when I couldn't avoid being in his physical presence (we did work in the same office after all), he continued to patronize my appearance with offhand remarks such as, "I like the way your glasses look on you," or "your hair looks nice today." Never did he state "that was a good idea," or "I like the approach you're taking on this issue." And moreover, he was careful to do this out of earshot of our colleagues. Sometimes he'd follow me out of a meeting and mumble something as he walked by in the hallway. To shift the focus from ME to the work at hand,

I would always counter by stating that, "The purpose of this meeting isn't to talk about my glasses/hair/outfit. It's to discuss Project X." After all, that was what we were there to discuss.

Additionally, he started a new tactic of leaving me in tricky situations where I was left with the task of doing damage control after his disruptive interactions with other colleagues. For example, during a call with our ad agency, *Harasshole* was repeatedly using profanity, which had become an everyday occurrence at this point. It was left to me to save the relationship with our vendor, as I was the one who had to address his actions with the members of the agency privately and apologize to their employees for his unprofessional behavior.

He was a senior leader, a member of the executive team, and expected to be an ambassador of the United Way brand and what it stood for. THIS is how he was representing the organization internally, and even worse, externally. This man was a walking disaster, plain and simple.

As time passed, *Harasshole's* provocations towards me intensified, both personally and professionally, as he continued his cheap commentary about my appearance and interrupted my work on a daily routine. It was clear that my silence was not going to make this hurricane pass.

Later that summer, I decided to share the offensive comments and numerous provocations with our HR Director, who was responsible for Employee Relations. I explained to her that I was uncomfortable raising a formal complaint against a peer but wanted her to have knowledge of the incidences. In confidence, she shared with me that I wasn't the first or the only one in the office who had already brought up complaints about his behavior. I had no reason, based on my own experiences, to even doubt others had complained. Cue the confused face emoji—why was this not being addressed? Why was he still a leader on the executive team? Why hadn't any action been taken to reprimand him? And if they had, he clearly wasn't taking it seriously. Why was I having to put up with this at all? I just wanted to do my job—after all, that's why I was there. And this was a distraction to me—to others—to organizational productivity. It needed to be addressed.

As summer ended, in September, we started gearing up for Dreamforce, a large annual conference scheduled for September 25-28 in San Francisco, where we would be in attendance with many of our staff members who were also scheduled to be there.

Harasshole extended an invitation to stay with him at the Airbnb he had rented for his team during the conference. NO WAY. Whatever his intentions were, I couldn't believe that he had the audacity to ask such an inappropriate question to a colleague. For male and female staff to stay together alone in a house only presented a potential liability to United Way. How could the organization allow this? Did they not comprehend the possible consequences of his actions? Were they even aware of what he was doing?

Confronted with yet another situation left me feeling nauseous; I emphatically declined and subsequently raised to HR via the same Director with whom I'd spoken earlier about the comments he'd been making, the liability United Way Worldwide faced by allowing him to domicile a co-ed team at the house. I had hoped that through my foresight, I had attempted to avoid a disaster. She promised to raise the issue to her executive team leader, the Chief Culture Officer.

Apparently, my concerns fell on deaf ears, and it happened anyway. The week after the conference, a young woman on *Harasshole's* team abruptly resigned from the organization without giving notice. Not surprisingly, while attending the conference, she stayed in the house he had rented.

It didn't take much for me to know something was off when I quickly learned that her resignation came with a severance package and that she had also signed an NDA. Getting a severance package when resigning isn't typically how it works. The EMPLOYEE is making a choice to leave in most resignations.

After she left United way, I had several private conversations with her, and while I will keep the details confidential, I will share that certain events at that house made her feel uncomfortable enough to bring it to HR. I'll let your imagination do the rest.

What I can say is, after I went public with my own story about *Harasshole*, I received a text message from her: "Proud of the strength it took to do this.... Three people shared your story with me because they know what happened to me. Thank you for speaking for all the women who had to suffer in silence."

Chapter 23

"Your strength doesn't come from winning. It comes from struggles and hardship. Everything that you go through prepares you for the next level."
Germany Kent

Six months before the drama in the office began, the American Marketing Association (AMA), the essential community for marketers, recognized our work to rebrand United Way and honored me with the 2017 Non-profit CMO of the Year Award, after a nomination I received from a local United Way CMO.

Undoubtedly this was one of the highlights of my professional career. While the award was singular and given only to me, it was indeed won by the efforts of my entire team. Our success continued to be recognized, and this was just the start of a long list of many awards that we as a team subsequently won. In 2017 alone, we won awards for our inaugural Digital Annual Report, PSA of the Year (from multiple sources), our Enterprise Twitter feed, our Annual Report, our Blog, and a Social Media Campaign promoting free tax preparation. I was also a nominee for the *Washington Business Journal's* CMO of the Year.

None of this is said with arrogance to impress you, but with pride of having the opportunity to lead an amazing team of individuals. It was a deliberate part of our marketing strategy, and it created great positive PR and helped United Way show up in new places where one wouldn't typically expect. I was so proud of all that my team had accomplished in under two years.

Winning the AMA award also opened the path for me to receive a nomination to join the AMA National Board. This was a unique and special honor, as I was the only non-academic non-profit professional to hold a seat on the board.

Later that October, on a trip to Chicago for an AMA board meeting, I learned from an acquaintance at the local United Way that *Harasshole* had also scheduled a trip to Chicago for a meeting at the United Way office, a mere fifteen-minute walk apart from the location of my AMA meeting. Oy vey! Was my hometown big enough for both of us?

I decided to take the bull by the horns (remember I grew up during the glory days of Michael Jordan) with the hope of building some kind of harmony between the two of us. Don't get me wrong—I didn't delude myself that we would ever create a cheerful environment. Nonetheless, I assumed that we might possibly be able to resolve our differences in the interest of improving our deteriorating business relationship. I even took the proactive step of informing the Chief Culture Officer of the meeting and she asked me to follow up on the outcome.

The selective optimist within me convinced the more pessimistic side of me to reach out to *Harasshole* and suggest a breakfast meeting. In my head, the idea of sharing a meal together in neutral territory could allow us to be open with each other and strive towards a positive working relationship. I really did believe deep in my heart that my effort to reach out would lead to a positive outcome.

Harasshole and I met at Wildberry Café for breakfast. I rarely eat breakfast, despite it being my favorite meal, thus

Chapter 23

I tended to reserve it for a weekday meeting (preferably with someone I actually liked) or for weekends and when I was on vacation.

The café was famous for its delicious homemade pancakes and offered organic products, cage free eggs, and oat milk before it was even a thing. He was a vegetarian -and practiced yoga. Strange, no? (You'd think a behemoth like him would be a meat eater to the core. Stereotypes aside, one would think of a yogi vegetarian as a more peaceful person), so I specifically found a place with a menu that included a wide range of breakfast options for the both of us to enjoy.

I strolled into the cafe early to secure a nice table in a quiet spot that would allow us to talk more freely. When he walked through the big glass revolving doors facing the Randolph Street entrance, I waved to catch his attention and greeted him with a genuine smile; I was ready to make a sincere attempt to bring down the barriers he began building from the very first day we met during the interview.

The face looking back at me was wearing a gloomy mask. The shadowed facade was a reliable sign that he was not going to play nice. There was no point in walking out of the restaurant, and I resolved to stick to my script and made the best of the situation. We sat in uncomfortable silence. The conversations around me felt like loud white noise.

Coffee came to our rescue as we awkwardly sat across from each other. Unfortunately, the infusion wasn't sufficient to save this morning, even with my attempts to make small talk as we perused the menu. By the time our food arrived, I had tried to start a conversation. But he ignored me, offered no response. He kept stirring his food around his plate, cutting it, and mushing it excessively to avoid any eye contact with me.

Then out of nowhere, he mumbled, "...everything is fucked up." Could this be the opening I was searching for to wipe the slate clean? I seized the opportunity and replied, "I'm sorry you're feeling that way. I'd like to know what I can do in the spirit of fostering a more positive working relationship between us. If I've done something to offend you, I'm not aware of it. I'd appreciate it if you'd please just tell me so I can address it." Zero response. Not a single word. We spent the rest of the meal in deafening silence.

I wolfed down my coveted breakfast in agony, paid the bill, and left in a loss for words. My wishful thinking that a freshly prepared breakfast would aid the conversation was clearly pointless. I extended an olive branch, but he didn't take it. I questioned myself what it was that I could have done differently. I later came to learn that this is a common tactic of those who endure harassment; we take on the blame, assuming WE must be the ones who cause this.

Chapter 24

"Good teams become great ones when the members trust each other enough to surrender the Me for the We."
Phil Jackson

As requested, after the Chicago trip, I scheduled a meeting with the Chief Culture Officer. In my email invitation, I noted that the intent was to discuss the outcome of my meet up with *Harasshole*. I also prepared a few notes to keep the discussion as objective as possible. When I arrived for my meeting to talk about the breakfast, she seemed uninterested in the topic, and to my dismay, she launched into a monologue about how she'd been screening candidates for the COO role we were hiring for but couldn't find the right one yet. "Nobody seemed to be a good match," she complained. "Really, this is happening?" I thought, "She's not going to address this situation at all? She was the one who had requested this meeting as a follow-up to the *Harasshole* issue." She didn't. The meeting passed with no mention, nor an opportunity for me to raise it before she hustled me out of her office.

To better understand the context, let's go back to the Hurricane *Harasshole* retreat back in July. The CEO had shared his idea of bringing the COO role back to the executive team. Currently, there was no one on the executive team who was leading an integrated business planning process or a strategic integration of various processes for efficiency. Despite the absence of this role, there were some labor and legal issues related to why the prior COO had left and why his position was then replaced with someone who carried the title of Chief Culture Officer, but that's not my story to tell.

During the discussion at the retreat, the group had mixed emotions about this controversial topic. We'd had high turnover in the executive team in recent years, and a year and a half into the role, I was already the third most tenured member on the senior staff. At the conclusion of the retreat, the CEO decided to hire a COO and tasked our Chief Culture Officer with the hiring.

Now that you understand the story of adding a COO back into the executive team, let's return to our regularly scheduled program of the post-Chicago meeting with the COO wannabe. She quickly turned the meeting into an opportunity to pitch herself as the candidate for the COO position and went on to explain her entire plan. In her view, with her existing responsibilities, she saw herself as the most suitable person for the role, and how she could effectively staff up an operations team to support her. She also knew that she couldn't execute her "well-thought" plan without the full support of her colleagues.

Peer interviews were a part of our interview process at United Way. The Chief of Staff and I had very different personalities and skill sets, which we both acknowledged made us a good team, so much so that we had previously interviewed many contenders jointly for various roles in the organization. I was looking forward to partnering with him once again to interview the COO candidates.

The Chief Culture Officer claimed that she'd already spoken to the rest of the group and that they all agreed with her idea. Apparently, I was the last one on her list, and she was confident she could count on my support, right?

I should take a moment now to state that one of my fundamental character flaws, which I'm working to improve (because we all have shit to fix), is extending trust on credit too quickly. I believe trust is one of the most important currencies in which we trade, and while YOU have to work hard to burn me, once you damage that trust, all bets are off. And if you want to regain my trust, you most likely will have to dedicate the rest of our time together to that. Unfortunately, I made a huge mistake when the COO tried to sell me her agenda that day. Nobody died, but it was a learning experience. Not only was I betrayed by someone whom I trusted, what made it worse given the scenario was that I was betrayed by a WOMAN, someone who herself had likely experienced this in the workplace, because after all, most of us have.

The Chief Culture Officer and I previously had had a good relationship. I didn't consider her a close friend, but we were friendly. On several occasions outside of work, we would spend time together in an effort to get to know one another better. She had relocated to D.C. for this job, but her family had not, leaving her without many acquaintances outside of work. Conveniently for both of us, she also lived right across the street from my hotel. We would often exercise together at the gym or would go out in the evening for a walk. Given my social circle in D.C. from my days at The UPS Foundation, I was often invited to events, and she used to regularly join me as my plus one.

We rarely talked business outside of the office, but I knew that she was well aware of what was occurring between myself and *Harasshole*.

Her betrayal made it clear to me that I was simply collateral damage in pursuit of her goals. She sold her soul to the devil to protect her benefactor, the CEO, even when she KNEW things were wrong. That in and of itself was one of the most disappointing things to me. She used to talk about family and faith, but at the end of the day, she was just a hypochristian who put on a false appearance of virtue and goodness while acting in contradiction to her stated beliefs. I lost all respect for her at that moment.

By the time we reached the holidays and neared the end of 2018, United Way underwent yet another slight tweak in the organizational chart, the aforementioned Chief Culture Officer was formally promoted to the Chief Operating Officer, and out of nowhere, *Harasshole* also received an internal "grade up" promotion with an Executive VP title, bringing him to true parity with me in terms of our levels.

Chapter 25

"You gain strength, courage and confidence by every experience in which... you are able to say to yourself, 'I lived through this horror. I can take the next thing that comes along.'..."
Eleanor Roosevelt

As 2018 ended, I was optimistic for a better 2019. Unfortunately, the reality sank in quickly, and the year started off worse than the one that had just come to an end. In January and February, nearly every face-to-face interaction with *Harasshole* included an inappropriate smirky comment about my physical appearance: "glasses look great on you, love your hair, the outfit is flattering on you...."

The thing that most people, including me at the time, do not realize about sexual harassment is that it's most often not about sex; it's about power: who has it and who does not.

The core concept is straightforward: everyone should be safe at work without fearing harassment, assault, or discrimination. Yet every day, more survivors come forward with horrific stories of what they have endured at work simply by trying to do their job and earn a living.

I frequently used to work late hours in the office since I was staying at a hotel during the week. However, as time went on, I started to become more aware and uneasy about his presence in the office. I began checking to figure out whether I was there alone or if he was still in the building after hours and when the rest of the group would be going home. I couldn't always tell for sure, but if I sensed he was still in the building or if I was uncertain if he had already left, I did not take any chances and took my work with me back to my hotel room. I wanted to avoid any possible situation where I may not be able to get out swiftly and would be alone with him in the office. I did not feel safe.

My frequent travel schedule required me to become an expert at packing. Out of a necessity to keep track of my dry cleaner rotation and my accessories, I developed a tracking system. Each weekend, after reviewing my calendar for the upcoming week's meetings and events, I packed a two-color palette outfit and no more than two pairs of shoes. I kept spreadsheets (I know, OCD, right? Just keep reading. . .) for what I wore each week to avoid repeating outfits. Hey, almost all the pieces in my wardrobe are entitled to the same attention and love.

In 2019, my OCD for keeping a spreadsheet of my outfits paid off when I had to attend a weeklong conference in cold Toronto, Canada. The heavy winter clothes broke my rule of not checking luggage when I exceeded my carry-on capacity. And as luck would have it, when I landed back in Atlanta, I couldn't locate my suitcase at the luggage carousel. Unfortunately, I never reunited with my belongings, but my packing list helped me immensely with the insurance claim. (To this day, I mourn the loss of my favorite black wool gabardine double breasted Ralph Lauren trench coat. It was military style with gold buttons, bold pockets, and fantastic stitching. I adored that coat.)

More seriously, though, another unexpected but important benefit of my list was that I was able to look back and better understand what I was wearing when *Harasshole* intensified his snarky comments about my appearance. In a situation like this, a typical course of action would be to "victim shame": she must have been wearing something to attract attention, or perhaps she was dressed inappropriately. I can tell you with a 110% degree of certainty, no, NEVER—and my list proves it. What I will say here is that even if I were wearing something that DID attract attention, it absolutely positively **does not** grant someone the right to comment on it in the workplace. Other than perhaps HR, if it is a violation of the dress code.

I take the workplace seriously, and professionalism is a hallmark of my personal brand. Anyone who knows me will attest to that. Professional dress, even in a business casual environment as we had is how I showed up. Each and every day. To me, it's a sign of respect for the workplace and the purpose for which I am there; to do work. Everyone has something they don't like about their body for me, my knees are my one insecurity. I do not like them, Sam I Am. I favor midi skirts, always below the knee at mid-calf. Not a single employee at United Way ever had the unfortunate fate of meeting my patellas. Nor do I own a v-neck or scoop neck shirt. What lies beneath my collarbone is a mystery. I am petite and curvy. That's not a sin, but I don't advertise it.

Although our offices were on different floors, and there was generally no reason for *Harasshole* to be by my office, he started to make a habit of creepily pacing back and forth past my door multiple times a day. On a random Thursday in mid-January 2019, he caught me as I walked out of my office, heading to Reagan International to fly home. He blatantly scanned my body up and down multiple times with what I assume was some salacious look of approval. "You look great today, Lisa. Really sharp. Nice."

I know damn well what I was wearing that day. For the record, it was a grey wool sweater dress by Theory: round neck, long sleeves, mid-calf length, ribbed wool with a white blouse under it, and black boots. Not fitted, not at all revealing. A suitable outfit in a workplace environment where the dress code essentially only forbid coming to the office in a bikini, pajamas, underwear, or barefoot.

I extricated myself, yet once again, from any interaction with him curtly, though still politely ignoring his comment, stating that I was in a hurry to catch my flight. The HR Director's office was a short three doors down from mine. At that point, I still hadn't filed a complaint, but I repeatedly had made the HR Director aware of these incidents. On my way to the elevator, I stopped in her office to inquire if she had perhaps overheard the exchange that had just occurred in the hallway. She had not, but I made her aware of what had just taken place. She just shook her head. That told me all I needed to know. Again. She was continuing to receive complaints, and nothing was being done to address this, "But why?" became my ongoing question at each one of these instances.

I now wondered if I really needed to file an official complaint. If they knew about it and it violated policy, shouldn't they have addressed it? Apparently not, as there would soon be a series of incidents that would be the proverbial "final straw"....

Chapter 26

"It is the last straw that breaks the camel's back."
Charles Dickens

A week into February of 2019, I was working late, and most of my team had already gone home. An administrative assistant on my team, Taylor, stopped by my office. She had done this before, as had others when they wanted some quiet time in private with me away from the prying eyes of others.

As we spoke, she innocuously tried to work into our conversation an incident with *Harasshole* several weeks prior. We had instituted an offsite happy hour event once a quarter at a local neighborhood watering hole where the employees could mix and mingle in a more social setting and build our internal culture. She shared with me that during the last event in late January or early February, *Harasshole* had "stalked her around the place and then slithered over to her" (her words, not mine) to strike up a conversation. Taylor obviously knew who *Harasshole* was due to his senior position in the company, but they had never actually interacted before.

During our conversation, Taylor reminded me of her recent application for a role on his team. I knew that her supervisor, a direct report to me, had alerted HR in early February when Taylor informed her about *Harasshole's* response to her application. She didn't want to go to HR directly, but his comment, "I'd love to see you working on my floor every day," made her uncomfortable.

Subsequently, I also alerted the VP of HR that I was aware of the situation as both the supervisor and the employee told me about this issue. By policy, if an employee reports an incident that made them uncomfortable, the person receiving that knowledge is obligated to report it to HR. And further, the supervisor had also brought it to my attention as the head of the department, and I was thus obligated to notify HR. Failure to do so could result in termination. This was no secret, for we all had had to go through harassment training just about six months prior.

This, of course, wasn't the only incident. A member of my team, a young LatinX LGBTQ female, reported to me that in a conversation with her, *Harasshole* had made distasteful remarks about wanting to punch Latinos who were expressing support for the current President of the United States (remember, this is 2019) in the face.

In both incidents, I stood up for my team members, both younger women of color who would not have filed an official complaint directly to HR about a white male C Suite Executive. Nevertheless, they knew that by telling their manager, even under the pretense of it being confidential and simply a "conversation," that it would end up in HR.

As I've said, 2019 didn't start off well. It was only the third week in February, and I had already been required to report multiple incidents involving my team and *Harasshole* to HR. The vague response from the VP of HR was that she had requested the COO to follow up with *Harasshole* was simply just not enough for me anymore. While I had been dealing with Harasshole's behavior towards me for nearly fifteen months, I hadn't yet officially gone to HR on my own behalf; only to protect the women on my team. There is no way they were going to take the risk of speaking out against a white male C-suite executive. But I could do it for them.

Here I was once again, being an upstander—standing up for what was right—but yet again, nothing happened. This was no longer just about me, but the members of my team, and this had to change. And it did.

The last straw came at the end of February during a United Way hosted internal conference at the beautiful Gaylord Hotel across the harbor from Alexandria. The evening before, I had attended a dinner with several of the local market CEOs who were in town for the conference... and *Harasshole*. Several long tables had been reserved at the restaurant for our large group, and fortunately, *Harasshole* and I were seated far away from one another. We had zero contact the entire evening, other than I could feel him staring at me, trying to catch my attention. I was lucky enough that I was able to ignore him the entire evening and left without saying a word. I was left to wonder, once again at the risk of sounding arrogant, what it was about me that triggered him to require constant interaction, a demand for my attention, a need to be noticed and in some way acknowledged by me.

By mid-morning on the first day of the conference, my luck ran out. The main session had just concluded, and a stream of people flooded the hallway, clustering around the refreshments. Coffee cups were being refilled, restroom breaks being taken, and attendees were checking their emails on mobile devices. There was a pleasant symphony of voices in the air—so far, so good. Yet as I stood at a high table outside the main ballroom lobby speaking with a female co-worker and another woman from a local United Way, I looked up and saw *Harasshole*. I did not want to start my day off with him. "It is too early in the morning for this," I thought.

He approached us from the diagonal, coming straight towards me, and again, very blatantly did a full body scan. Head to toe and then back up again. After what seemed like an eternity, he made eye contact as his gaze rose to the level of my face. I felt like a fish in a glass bowl. Things quickly went south from there. In front of the two women with whom I had been speaking before he interrupted he stated, in his typical tone of voice, "That skirt looks great on you, fits you nice."

Again, I know what I was wearing: a black sweater with a big white bow at the neck, a multi-colored vertically striped midi skirt, and black boots. Not an inch of skin to be seen. The skirt wasn't tight because of a sequin overlay that would have left a trail of sparkles in my wake if it were fitted and pulled at all.

A flush of embarrassment flooded across my cheeks. My heart hammered, and my internal temperature rose with shame. It was awful enough that I had already endured this humiliating nonsense countless times one-on-one in the office, but now he was extending this torture in front of an audience. Although not direct reports to either of us, these women were still employed by United Way. He was disrespectful to me in front of these women. How dare he! I felt reduced to an object, not as a valued asset of the leadership team. I was mortified and embarrassed beyond belief.

Stumbling over my words and struggling to maintain composure, I apologized to the women that they had to witness this behavior. My coworker blew it off. Honestly,

Chapter 26

I was disappointed in her response, "That's just *Harasshole*." She accepted his behavior and brushed it off. Given the power imbalance that the white male patriarchy holds, this was disappointing but not altogether surprising. Often, I've seen women make excuses for this type of behavior and simply accept it as part of a personality trait. Let me be clear—a personality trait, disorder, whatever, this is not okay, and there should be no tolerance or acceptance of this. This demonstrated a lack of leadership on his part, and since we had recently completed mandatory sexual harassment training, he knew better.

What really went down when no one was watching was one thing. But this was the first time he had harassed me, this obviously in front of someone else. Some of my team members had seen and commented on *Harasshole* looking for me when I wasn't in my office or making them uncomfortable with how they saw him looking at me. Generally speaking, the tone was that he was just "creepy." But now, he had escalated the situation to a new low.

Chapter 27

"Above all, be the heroine of your life, not the victim."
Nora Ephron

Let's reaffirm here once again: sexual harassment is about POWER. In this case, while we were peers, *Harasshole* attempted to take *my* power by putting me into an awkward and embarrassing situation in front of other employees who became bystanders -- excusing his behavior and what he did as simply just part of his persona.

Read these two statements—and consider how they are different.

1. "I like your outfit today."
2. "That skirt looks great on you. It fits you nicely."
   Accompanied by a leer.

When a man mentions how a female co-worker's outfit FITS her, I'm here to tell you, that it is <u>NOT</u> OKAY. When he does it ALL THE TIME, it is <u>NOT</u> OKAY.

Sexual harassment in the workplace is illegal under Title VII of the Civil Rights Act and is defined as a type of harassment involving the use of explicit or implicit sexual overtones, including the unwelcome and inappropriate promise of rewards in exchange for sexual favors, sexual harassment includes a range of actions from verbal transgressions to sexual abuse or assault.

The inclusion of verbal transgressions is key; many people mistakenly assume that for sexual harassment to occur, it must be in the form of a physical interaction. Verbal transgressions are indeed and most definitely a form of sexual harassment.

In 1986, a U.S. labor law case, *Meritor Savings Bank v. Vinson*, saw the United States Supreme Court, in a nine to zero decision, recognize sexual harassment as a violation of Title VII of the Civil Rights Act of 1964. The case was the first of its kind to reach the Supreme Court and redefined sexual harassment in the workplace. It established the standards for analyzing whether the conduct was unlawful and when an employer would be liable. The court, for the first time, made sexual harassment an illegal form of discrimination.

After that encounter with *Harasshole* at the conference, I was a wreck for the rest of the day. Trying to keep a brave face on and fight back the tears was nearly impossible, and physically, my stomach was twisting and turning. Luckily, I didn't cross paths with *Harasshole* again for the rest of the day—not that it mattered, the damage was done.

Again, I just couldn't put this particular encounter out of my mind. While this was not new behavior, this instance appeared to be an escalation in his bravado driven by confidence in the fact that there hadn't to date and likely wouldn't be any accountability for his ongoing inappropriate, and candidly, illegal behavior. In an effort to distance myself from him, I checked out of the Gaylord and relocated to my usual Sheraton by the office. I would Uber to return to the conference venue in the morning. I didn't want to get caught alone with him, and the hotel just didn't feel safe any longer. I needed distance from him and, quite frankly, the whole situation. I left the hotel in tears trembling, and took an Uber back across the harbor. The disrespect I had been shown was inexcusable. I was his peer, a leader in the organization, and he had just reduced my worth to nothing more than how my physical appearance was pleasing to him—objectifying me—and marginalizing me in front of two colleagues.

Chapter 28

"Your silence will not protect you."
Audre Lorde

That evening, to document the incident in writing, I emailed the female co-worker who had witnessed *Harasshole's* comments firsthand and apologized for my reaction to *Harasshole's* comments about my skirt. Her almost immediate reply was, "Thank you so much, Lisa. I'm grateful for our partnership in general and always appreciate your candor and insight. We all have days... or weeks :) Much love and respect to you."

I wasn't sure what to make of her response other than the fact that *Harasshole* was a white male C-Suite leader, and perhaps she felt that any acknowledgment of his behavior, no matter how vile, would lead to unsolicited trouble for her. After all, she had seen how he treated me, and why on earth would she want to put herself at risk to become a target? Maybe it was because she reported to the COO and didn't want to get sideways there. I have no clue and cannot blame her. What I do know is this is a classic example of being a bystander and watching the events unfold while also being unsure of how to productively intervene.

About an hour after my email exchange with the female co-worker, the Chief of Staff called me to follow up on a video project for the CEO. He must have heard the distress in my voice as he asked if I was okay. "Yeah, just a little headache," I replied, trying to fight back the tears, but I couldn't swallow this absurdity any longer. There was so much I kept to myself. Tears slid down my face like raindrops on a windshield as I leaned against the door jamb separating the bedroom from the bathroom. "Well, no, not really," I added. He calmly said, "I didn't think so."

I initially hesitated to share with him what had happened that day but then decided to seek his guidance. I never complained about *Harasshole* to those reporting to me. Other than HR and a few selected peers, I kept my frustrations to myself. As I described what happened, his tone became a bit uneasy. He agreed *Harasshole's* behavior needed to stop as he muttered "Oh, that guy...."

We debated the pros and cons of sharing this with the COO and decided against it. We were all peers, and this could put her in an awkward position. The truth is, we honestly didn't think she'd address it anyway. He recommended I speak with the VP of HR, who was a direct report to the COO.

The following morning, I met with the VP of HR privately in my office behind closed doors. I knew *Harasshole* was across the water. Desperate for peace that never came, I shared my perspective about his ongoing behavior. I broke down in tears when I had to share that the day before, he crossed a line when he did it in front of others. The rest was bad enough on its own, but now... it was unbearable. He'd done it once, he'd continue to push boundaries. Like a child seeing how far they can go before getting in trouble.

She was empathetic (somewhat) and stated she'd address it with him. I started to get nervous—this was now, once and for all, out in the open. It was "official;" I'd gone to HR. Was

Chapter 28

he going to ramp up the retaliation or escalate in another manner?

The following week I received an email from her confirming that she had spoken with him, and instructing me to notify her of any change in behavior from him. She had also informed the COO and felt that "...after talking to her that this is more than inappropriate; this is not a behavior you or anyone else should ever experience."

I felt some relief as I read her words on my screen. It was short-lived.

Chapter 29

"It actually doesn't take much to be considered a difficult woman. That's why there are so many of us."
Jane Goodall

Things remained quiet as February rolled into March, well, maybe for just a minute or two....

While on set filming our latest round of TV spots in mid-March, the CEO called me out of the blue to inform me that he was moving the digital marketing team that I had been responsible for leading over to *Harasshole*.

For the first of multiple times in that call, he also told me that I needed to "get rid" of my direct report, the Vice President who had gone to HR on behalf of her two employees. Shocked with this direct ask, I inquired if he was aware of the conversations that I had had to have with HR regarding *Harasshole's* behavior towards me and others. He answered, "Yes," and added, "you and your girls need to get along with him." I explained that this was not about us not getting along. It was about his unacceptable behavior that candidly put the organization at risk. He did not care. He simply did not want to hear it.

At the end of March 2019, the entire organization received a notice that United Way had revised its sexual harassment policy. Even though we had just had training roughly six months prior, all employees were required to attend the mandatory training. I thought this was odd, but since there hadn't been really any penalty for *Harasshole*, it never crossed my mind that this may have been the organization trying to protect itself. Stage whisper: "That's okay—don't worry about your employees and what this is doing to them...."

March seamlessly melted into April. On April 2, only two weeks after the initial directive to terminate my employee who had reported *Harasshole* to HR, the topic arose again. However, this time it was during a live meeting. The CEO told me I needed to shift marketing to a digital organization and focus on data. He added that he didn't care about any workload or staffing challenges to accomplish this. He tersely added, "Your (Direct Report)'s gotta go." I felt stuck between a rock and a hard place.

Virginia is an "At-Will" employment state which means employers can let go of employees at will, without reason or notice. I had no cause to terminate her—she had been my top performer for two years. In all honesty, I told the CEO that I believed she would probably throw in the towel and resign within the next six months anyway due to her frustration over this entire situation. He responded that it was too long to wait and began incorrectly citing negative characterizations attributed to her, which I in turn tried to rectify.

Life probably would have been much easier for me at work if I had given in to the CEO's power play and fired this employee without questioning the reasoning or motivation behind it. However, I knew that this would have been the wrong thing to do. Every morning when I get up, the face that looks back at me in the mirror is mine. I have to live with myself and the decisions I make. Without a single doubt, I knew in my heart that terminating an employee for no legitimate reason was wrong. I was determined not to go down that path. I wasn't going to do it, so I kept on fighting.

Two days after the CEO's second request to terminate my employee and just short of ten days after the initial conversation about *Harasshole*, on April 4, 2019, I had my annual employee performance review with my boss, the CEO. This was for my 2018 year-end review.

When I started with United Way in late 2015, the review system was on a five-point star system. However, since the COO joined the team in 2016, the employee performance key measures and grading methods at the non-profit had undergone a series of changes for the annual and mid-year reviews.

The organization had now migrated to three categories and rated them as "exceptional, solid, or emerging," which were as follows:

1. <u>Work Plan</u>: Did the employee accomplish and deliver what they were supposed to?
2. <u>Competencies</u>: Did the employee have the right skill sets for the roles and demonstrate them satisfactorily?
3. <u>Cultural Behaviors</u>: Did the employee exhibit the values the organization expected?

I had never thought much about the employee performance review. Suffice it to say, my performance had always been exemplary across the board. I regularly received above average ratings from my boss and peers, and I felt that I consistently delivered what was expected. The comments on my latest review dated November 6, 2018, were all positive, and I continued my performance consistently until the end of the year. So for this next review, I was expecting nothing less. Here is my rating:

Work Plan: Exceptional. Same as last year. I expected this rating since there was no disputing the fact that I had not only delivered my goals but exceeded expectations.
Competencies: Solid. Downgraded from exceptional to solid.
Culture: Solid. I had maintained my previous year's rating.

Why was I downgraded in Competencies from exceptional to solid? How did my feedback rating get downgraded since November? What changed so drastically? His positive comments from the November review were still fresh and recent in my mind.

Deep down, while I didn't fully realize it at the time, this was the onset of a systemic pattern of retaliation that I would have to endure, I did understand that something was "off." I had a consistent three-year record of good performance. I knew something was wrong, considering he had never before provided any sort of constructive feedback or criticism. More importantly, there was no commentary or response to my inquiries about where I had fallen short. I asked for specifics and was given nothing other than a few vague answers. I was told that I needed to operate in a culture of ambiguity and learn to lead a data-driven organization.

My boss told me that I had fallen short on data-driven management. This was not a stated competency, nor anything we'd even talked about previously. Regardless, I led the organization's research team and had numerous data points for all the work I had conducted in order to prove that I wasn't making decisions out of my backside. He knew very

Chapter 29

well that my recommendations to him were always based on data.

As I pushed for more answers, the ugly truth started to slowly work its way to the surface as my boss continued his monologue. He felt like I was "documenting" and recording my review, and he didn't appreciate that. He ended the review by telling me to stop looking back at the previous year (this is my 2018 review!!!) and to start looking forward and discussing what I will or should be doing and how I was going to deliver what I had promised regarding the new direction. Remember, I was notified of this new direction only TWO DAYS earlier, literally forty-eight hours ago, almost to the minute before my review for the previous year.

Chapter 30

"Fight for the things that you care about, but do it in a way that will lead others to join you."
Ruth Bader Ginsburg

After my review that day, my assistant flew into my office for the express purpose of telling me about a weird encounter she had just had with *Harasshole*. She was Black and sometimes wore her hair in braids. *Harasshole* approached her, picked up one of her braids, looked at it, and then made a comment about how good her hair looked. I asked if it bothered her, and she replied that it was "creepy, but that's just *Harasshole*." (Again, readers, this is NOT okay!)

It was another situation in which *Harasshole's* behavior was dismissed as simply being part of his persona. I told her that "just *Harasshole*" wasn't an acceptable excuse for such behavior because clearly, it bugged her enough to come into my office and tell me about it. She agreed.

I could not understand for the life of me how or why this was able to continue happening. Touching anyone, even their hair, at work, especially someone with whom you have zero personal relationship is inappropriate. It's inappropriate even if you DO have a personal connection. I'd find it odd if a colleague close to me, male or female, physically touched my hair. In return, I would never touch them either.

The following week during a conversation with the COO, for the first time, I directly stated that I felt both my direct report and I were being targeted for raising issues about *Harasshole*. In turn, she quickly got very defensive, "No, the issues with your direct report are bigger." (Again, people, NOT okay as a response).

The COO seemed a bit surprised when I shared with her the CEO's directive to shift to a data-driven organization and to "get rid of" my direct report, as well as how I was told to get along with *Harasshole*. I told her that the intelligence I had conducted absolutely refuted what the CEO had alleged. For example—he told me my employee had asked "weird questions in an interview." First and foremost, he wasn't even in the interview; it was for a role on my team for which my direct report had conducted a peer interview. The Chief of Staff had been present at the interview and validated that the questions were about process and project management and not "weird" at all. Plus, if there had been pervasive issues with my direct report, as her manager, someone would have and should have brought it to my attention so that I could have addressed them. No one had ever raised any complaints about her to me, her manager.

Chapter 31

"The World produces waves. Surf or drown. You decide."
Virgil Abloh

As the weather warmed up, the incidents at the office began to heat up as well. At the end of April, the entire executive team, including me, was at our Global Conference in Toronto, Canada. For some reason, I was uninvited by the President of the U.S. division to a meeting she was hosting with a number of local CEOs where the other members of the executive team would all be present. She offered no explanation other than I just wasn't needed. From that point forward, I essentially spent the rest of the conference frozen out of participating in any part of it. I was largely ignored by the executive team and the CEO. I had actually, in partnership with the Chief of Staff, developed the format and programming for this conference—why was I being excluded?

After that event, I recall telling the COO that I felt like I had been deliberately excluded from key meetings with our network CEOs. She made a lame excuse that didn't even pass the blush test for a full-on attempt to cover it up.

I had been *friendly* but never "friends" with my co-workers. Since the issue with the COO, I now intentionally kept my co-workers at arm's length regarding my private life. That's not to say that I completely isolated myself socially from others. The Chief Development Officer had forgotten to bring a prescription she needed on the trip to the Global Conference, and since she lived close to me in Atlanta, her husband ran it over to me so that I could bring it to her in Toronto. Once I arrived, she came to my hotel room to pick it up. While she camped out in my room with a glass of wine she had brought with her, we ended up talking for quite a while. I still had my guard up when I was around others and continued to distance myself from personal interactions, but I lent her a friendly ear.

The conversation somehow led to *Harasshole*. She, too, had tangled with him as well, though in a different way—strictly business as far as I know—and had complained about him multiple times to me. She had also witnessed his disastrous outburst back in July at the breakout session during the retreat since we had been on the same sub-team.

As the conversation deepened, she shared with me that she had expressed a concern to the COO about a female on her team who was interested in a role on *Harasshole's* team. She told the COO that she was afraid his behavior with this woman would result in her filing a sexual harassment suit. OH MY GOD! It wasn't just me! I thought to myself in relief. Yet a few weeks later, however, the woman who was the subject of that discussion was moved to *Harasshole's* team, directly reporting to him.

Shortly thereafter, early that summer, the HR Director told me that she felt things "weren't right," sharing that it had been brought to her attention that during a recent meeting with his staff, *Harasshole* had told one of his male employees to "man-up and stop being a p*ssy." In front of the entire team. Who talks like that? At work, no less. She shared in confidence with me that she had received many complaints about him, investigated and turned in a report to the COO. Despite the fact that she was responsible for overseeing Employee Relations, the COO had blocked all of her attempts to work with and coach *Harasshole*. Instead, she was essentially told to "back off," and in June, shortly after she turned in the investigation report to the COO, she was terminated.

It was at that moment when I realized that since my formal complaint to HR in February about *Harasshole's* behavior, the following had occurred, for which I have listed the events below:

- I received a poor performance review with no supporting evidence, not in line with prior reviews.
- Resources were taken from my team and re-allocated to *Harasshole*, including the employee who had reported some of the initial complaints to HR. HR was aware of this yet sent her to his team.
- I'd been instructed on multiple occasions to terminate an employee who had also complained.
- I'd lost resources, but no responsibility had been removed. I was not allowed to replace resources (we had a hiring freeze, but I was not allowed to replace a single position, yet *Harasshole* and others were).
- I was consistently taken off the agenda for meetings and had no visibility with the board even though I had previously presented to them each quarter.

Chapter 32

"If you want to be liked by everyone, you have to die today. Because while you speak the truth, more will dislike you than like you."
Anand Mehrotra

As summer of 2019 closed, I had my mid-year performance review via phone with the CEO on August 28, the day before I departed for a much-needed vacation in Cambodia. During the conversation, he told me, "Your year is going great. I notice you're reaching out, especially to *Harasshole*. I feel good about where you are."

I was starting to think I was losing my mind. It was almost as if he was deliberately trying to keep me off balance. A typical demonstration of the practice known as "gaslighting," where someone psychologically manipulates someone into questioning their own sanity or reality. He never acknowledged all, or even any of the issues with *Harasshole*—it seemed as though by ignoring it, he was willing it to cease to exist. Maybe he could make me think it was all in my head, or never really happened; I have no idea why he commented about my reaching out to *Harasshole*. If anything, that showed character on my part—problem resolution, conflict management, etc. Perhaps an exemplary showing of how hard I was trying to address and manage a situation that had been thrust upon me and everyone else was blatantly ignoring.

I really needed that trip. And I wish I could have gifted one to my team, too; they were drowning. We had lost resources to *Harasshole*, yet the work stayed with us. Morale was low, and we were battling with *Harasshole's* team on a frequent basis as they blatantly disregarded brand, marketing, and communications protocols for which we were responsible and went rogue. We had an organizational hiring freeze—at least for my team. People began to quit, and I couldn't replace them. For my colleagues, especially *Harasshole*, other people miraculously seemed to be able to bring on the resources they needed. We spent a lot of time we didn't have cleaning up the messes created by *Harasshole's* team, presumably at his direction. I felt bad as a leader. The work needed to get done, and only had few people to do it—any capacity to solve this had effectively been curtailed. It didn't matter how many thank you notes I wrote, pizzas I bought, or work I personally took on to try and make it better for them. We all knew what was happening, and it sucked. For all of us.

After my trip, in late September, the COO requested that I speak to a coach whom United Way had engaged in supporting *Harasshole*. Why was United Way investing money in him and also taking my time to try and assist him? Why was he my problem to fix? This was getting ridiculous.

I detested the position I was put into. Most likely, if a man on the team were asked and said, "No, I'm too busy," no one would perceive this in a negative way, but I didn't want to risk finding myself in the middle of a contentious view yet again.

Even though I was not comfortable with the idea of meeting with the coach, I was worried that if I didn't cooperate, this whole thing would eventually blow back on me. I didn't want to be perceived as difficult and not a good team player who wasn't willing to try her best to resolve the issues. Somehow, his issues appeared to take precedence over mine, which weren't even acknowledged. He was being coached, counseled—I was left on my own to deal with the emotional damage he was wreaking on me. This is a common mistake employers make when trying to protect themselves; fix the problem child, so there's no complaint they didn't help, but those who were impacted (because I refuse to use the word "victim") are left to their own devices. Did anyone ask what help I needed or how I was feeling as a result of his actions towards me? Hell, no.

For better or worse, in the end, I felt I had no other choice but to agree to one last hurrah. I set a meeting date with the coach at a Starbucks so that *Harasshole* wouldn't see me in the office with him. Admittedly, I still had a last ray of hope that this could bring a much-needed sense of order back into my work life.

Despite my willingness, it seemed like the work with the coach was not bearing any fruit. For a while now, *Harasshole* had been stoking distrust between our teams, creating a wedge between them, even speaking poorly about us to his team, which all started to seep back to my team members. To make matters worse, the strain this caused between our two teams began to impact performance and interfere with clients. By that October, the incidents with *Harasshole* had continued to pile up.

Case in point: One morning at the airport before a flight to Chicago, I had to be on a conference call with *Harasshole* to resolve a few business issues. And in true fashion, his behavior was what can only be described as passive aggressive bullying. As soon as I landed at Midway Airport

I called the COO, still feeling an overwhelming sense of frustration from the morning call, and I shared with her that I was starting to experience anxiety issues from the stress he was causing. I had an elevated heart rate, stomach pains, and trouble sleeping.

Parroting the CEO, she preached to me (echoing the exact same words spoken by the CEO back in March) that "I needed to learn to get along with *Harasshole*" and that she, along with the VP of HR, would "investigate" and get back to me. As I later found out from my team members, when the COO and VP of HR spoke to them, the positioning was that I was the one causing issues with *Harasshole*. Apparently, the CEO told them to look into this.

I emailed *Harasshole's* coach and canceled our upcoming meeting, stating that I had gone to HR once again since we had last spoken and that I was not comfortable continuing our discussions.

In the October executive team meeting to review the annual Employee Engagement Survey results, the CEO again called for an unwarranted dismissal of my direct report—in front of my colleagues. With an audience watching this time, things were not as simple. In six months, this was the third occasion where he directed me to terminate a top-performing employee who coincidentally happened to be the one who initially raised issues about *Harasshole* to HR.

The reality was there was zero substantiation for the termination of this employee beyond random comments from the CEO that the employee was "bad for culture," with nothing to back such accusations. I had now been put on the spot in front of my peers to respond to him on this. Given the circumstances, knowing that they were not going to allow me to replace the resources I had lost in the past, I told him I would agree to the termination as long as I could hire a replacement. As expected, I was told no. Now the entire executive team had visibility into this. I hoped this would tip the balance of the scale.

Chapter 33

"It is better to lead from behind and put others in front especially when you celebrate victory when nice things occur. You take the front line when there is danger. Then people will appreciate your leadership."
Nelson Mandela

As everything continued to unfold, I had lunch with a friend who was a former employment attorney living in D.C. We knew each other from our UPS days.

Over lunch, I shared with her everything that had been going on at the office. She listened patiently. "You probably need an attorney," she said quietly, leaning across the table. As I nodded in agreement, I asked for a few trusted referrals to have in my back pocket.

In retrospect, one mistake I had made was not engaging legal counsel at that point or filing with the Equal Employment Opportunity Commission (EEOC), this federal agency established via the Civil Rights Act of 1964 to administer and enforce civil rights laws against workplace discrimination. The EEOC investigates discrimination complaints based on an individual's race, color, national origin, religion, sex, age, disability, sexual orientation, gender identity, genetic information, and retaliation for reporting, participating in, and/or opposing a discriminatory practice.

Despite the emotional chaos I had to live with Monday through Friday, a proud moment came my way that October when *Target Marketing* magazine notified me that I had been selected as their "Marketer of the Year." The December edition was going to include a feature on me—I always wanted to be a Cover Girl.

The magazine suggested sending a photographer to the office and interviewing people who had worked with me along the way. My immediate reaction, however, was to keep this hidden, even though the truth was that I shouldn't have had to hide the photoshoot—this was a big WIN for United Way. But it was not viewed that way; all of the awards that my team had racked up were now objects of envy. People were saying that this was all about building recognition for me.

Anyone who knows me can attest to the fact that I am genuinely not driven by ego. This wasn't about ME. This was part of a deliberate strategy my team and I had jointly developed and implemented, with the knowledge and approval from the CEO. Pursuing awards for UNITED WAY, not LISA BOWMAN, was an effective way to create positive public relations opportunities that didn't exist yet and increase the visibility for the non-profit.

The truth was, I had zero inkling about the *Target Marketing* magazine award until they notified me. When the editorial piece was published, it stated, "*Target Marketing* editors chose Bowman after sifting through nominations from readers, editors, editorial board members, and marketing thought leaders...."

By now, I knew that every time accolades were bestowed on my team for our success, it would stoke a benzene fire in *Harasshole*. And furthermore, the CEO was also accustomed to being the only one out there as the face of

Chapter 33

the organization. Deep down, I suspected he probably didn't like it, but again, it was not about ME—it was about the TEAM; it was about raising more funds to help more people in need.

I didn't want them to speak with him about me and the award I would be receiving. I didn't trust him not to be so petty to think this was self-promotion on my part. To avoid the possibility of this happening, I instead asked the Chief of Staff.

Chapter 34

"Being a good person does not mean you have to put up with other people's crap."
Anonymous

By early November, my multiple inquiries about the progress of the supposed "investigation" had all been unanswered, so I called for a meeting with the COO and VP of HR. In it, they delivered their cold conclusion: "it was shared blame" and offered no specifics. I was shocked. How on earth could they feel as though *Harasshole's* behavior could be waved off as an issue we were both at fault over? I did not understand or agree with their conclusion, but I tried to accept that perhaps I should own something and try to fix it. This is a very common reaction with sexual harassment and hostile environment workplaces. Oftentimes, the victim feels as though they should share their portion of the blame, even if they did nothing wrong.

While they had not yet spoken with *Harasshole*, they had already shared their findings with the CEO. I requested that the COO and VP of HR help facilitate a conversation between *Harasshole* and me in order to mediate our relationship to a better place. Their response was to ignore my requests repeatedly, with excuses about why they couldn't speak to him and bring us together. To the best of my knowledge, the results of their "investigation" were never addressed with *Harasshole* even though they claimed they had been and were not able to substantiate it in subsequent legal responses.

A series of strange events followed that, upon reflection, were all tied to the systemic pattern of retaliation I experienced for reporting *Harasshole* to HR and refusing to terminate an employee without cause.

First, my assistant, who had complained about *Harasshole* touching her hair, had long been a well-documented performance issue. After more than a year of coaching and counseling her, by early November, I was left with no alternative but to place her on an improvement plan with the help of both the COO and VP of HR.

She was notified of being placed on a Performance Improvement Plan on a Monday, and that Tuesday, I traveled to Albuquerque, New Mexico, where I was meeting with the local United Way to assist them with their marketing plan at the request of their CEO, whom I knew well.

On Wednesday, while I was away, my assistant unexpectedly resigned, directly to the COO and then to me. I later became aware that she sent an email to another employee stating that the COO asked her at the time of her resignation "if she could just hold on until January." The COO obviously knew at that point what plans were in the works to eliminate me. She also shared with that same employee that the VP of HR also told her at that time, "Don't worry, we'll take care of Lisa."

Our early December executive team meeting began with the CEO stating that he was thinking about hiring a Chief Experience Officer to aggregate all customer facing work which currently fell under me, *Harasshole*, and our Chief

Chapter 34

Development Officer. He was going to schedule time with each of us the following week to get our thoughts on it.

When I met with him the following week, I expressed interest in the role, as I knew that this was the new direction most CMOs were going in. I reminded him that I had been asking for additional opportunities and/or an expanded scope for nearly two years at this point. With as close as he ever got to humor, or perhaps it was just thinly disguised sarcasm, he acknowledged that there would be an issue if either *Harasshole* or I had to report to one another.

One week after that conversation, the CEO requested to speak with me. He informed me that he had hired someone for the Chief Experience Officer, and that both *Harasshole* and myself would now both report to the new hire. It had been nearly two weeks since that initial conversation, where we first discussed his desire to create this new position. Now someone had already been hired? Suspicious. You don't make a hire at that level in two weeks; this must have been in the works for quite some time.

I was scheduled to be on vacation but had to cancel my plans when a last-minute work issue came up. The entire executive team was supposed to be all hands-on-deck to make calls to the 1000 United Way CEOs about a last minute dues increase across the United Way network. Still, somehow, the COO took her scheduled time off and was unavailable during this "critical" business issue, even though I was forced to forfeit my vacation time. Clearly, she was in the CEO's pocket and had sold her soul for the job.

My mind wandered back to the information I'd received when my assistant resigned. "Can you just hold out until January," and

"Don't worry, we'll take care of Lisa." It became clear this had been in the works at least as far back as early November.

I inquired if the three of us would still be members of the executive team as direct reports to this new person. His seemingly surprising response was that he believed so but would ponder it over the holidays. Great, now I gave up my vacation AND would spend the holidays worrying about what this meant for my career.

The week of Christmas (!) the executive team received the following email from the CEO:

> "Good morning, folks. I wanted to formally announce that we have hired [John Doe], President [Company] Foundation, as our new Chief Experience Officer. I'm very excited about this addition to our leadership team. [John Doe] brings the type of capability and experience that we were looking for in this critical position. I've attached his resume for your review. I realize that adding someone to this position will affect the entire team. I'm very conscious of that fact but believe that [John Doe] will make us stronger. He will begin the first week in February. This will give us all of January, including our retreat, to plan for his arrival and to integrate him and the function into our work.
>
> We won't make any other internal or external announcements until after the first of the year. I thought it is necessary, however, that you know."

I spent the holidays stressed and worried. My husband and I were in one of my favorite places, Southern California, but I couldn't relax—I had a new boss, which is always nerve wracking. What did this all mean? I decided to be proactive and reach out to him since he made the announcement. I

Chapter 34

sent a sincere message on LinkedIn congratulating him on joining the team and telling him I was looking forward to working with him.

Happy New Year, 2020! Who knew what the year would have in store for all of us shortly? I certainly had NO idea what it held in store for me, but I would quickly find out.

Chapter 35

"If you're going through hell, keep going."
Winston Churchill

Because of how the holiday fell, New Year's Day 2020 was on a Wednesday, so I headed back to Alexandria on Monday, January 6. Stepping back into the routine that kept me grounded as I began my fifth year of living away from home during the week, I headed down to DryBar on King Street early Tuesday morning for my 7 a.m. blowout, accompanied by a Starbucks' grande soy latte.

As I left DryBar forty-five minutes later feeling good with my bouncy hair, I received the following text from the CEO, "Good morning, Lisa. I hope you had a great holiday. I'm going to have my assistant find us a time to talk this week to follow up on our year-end conversation. Thanks."

The text was followed up shortly with a calendar invite for Thursday, January 9 at 1:30 p.m.—two days later. My curiosity was piqued, my nerves shot, but I had no clue anything was truly amiss. There was nothing to "worry" about, right? I'd finished my year with strong visible results once again. I'd been recognized by an industry leading publication as their "Marketer of the Year." And perhaps, this new person, apparently my new "boss" would quickly open his eyes and see what was happening with *Harasshole*. Maybe the CEO was even looking for him to be the "cleanup guy," so he didn't have to do it, given he'd been so willfully ignorant about the behavior.

On Thursday, with a bit of apprehension, I walked the one hundred feet from my office to the CEO's. His office had a lovely corner view of the Potomac; you could see the Capitol Rotunda, and very often, we'd see Marine One flying by or a squadron of Blackhawks.

When I entered, he motioned me to sit down. Without preamble or any inquiry into how my holiday break had been (or my husband's cancer removal surgery of which he was aware), the CEO launched into a monologue about his holiday spent at his recently purchased beach house on Hilton Head Island, South Carolina. For ten minutes, he went on about his family, his new place, his holiday. "Why am I here?" I wondered.

Then, BAM! "Lisa, I'm going to be direct with you. I don't need you."

WHAT? In that moment that had instantly transformed into a nightmare, I tried to remain strong and professional. "DO NOT CRY. DO NOT CRY," I kept telling myself over and over again. Nope, not going to happen! My eyes exploded with tears, and I quickly covered my face, completely embarrassed. I blinked, uncertain yet certain of what I'd just heard. That feels like such a stereotypical female response and one that I hated myself for at that moment. But it happened, the tears came, and I couldn't hold them back. I felt myself go numb... in shock. Had I just lost my job??? Why? I'd NEVER been fired. EVER. From ANYTHING.

Honestly, at the time, I was not even completely sure that I was being fired. There was no HR representative present, no witness, no discussion regarding performance-related issues, and not even a prepared severance package. He

Chapter 35

never even mentioned anything regarding termination or actually being fired. I pulled myself together long enough to stumble through a few questions. There had never been any performance issue or other issue so, why was I being fired? Was there some type of severance package?

The cold, blunt answers I received were, "The new guy (Chief Experience Officer) will be my guy now. (Note the language from someone whom by now I fully recognized as a total misogynist; "My guy.")" and "Get with HR and 'work out the details.'"

I raised the fact that "his guy" and I had different skills. His core competencies and experiences were tech aligned, akin to *Harasshole's*. Was there still not a role for me here? The emphatic answer I received from my now apparently former boss was, "No. No. NO. There's no role for you here."

He then proceeded to make some inane comments about needing to eliminate my travel expenses associated with the fact that I commuted from Atlanta. This had never been raised as a concern and seemingly came out of nowhere. Wait just a minute! His "guy" ironically also lived in Atlanta. And moreover, only four of the nine members of the executive team lived locally; the remaining five commuted to D.C from other locations, including Atlanta, Tampa, and New Hampshire. Did they raise the cost as a concern with them as well? I inquired if "his guy" was going to be commuting. Apparently, without his brain and mouth connecting, the answer was "Yes, for about eighteen months, then he'll relocate."

I walked out of his office like a zombie, with plenty of visible evidence on my face that I had been crying. His executive assistant kindly asked if I was okay, and I mechanically feigned that I was fine.

I sat in my office, which was, unfortunately, adjacent to his, as my mind walked through all the effort I had given to this role, and all the sacrifices I had made for this company. The weekly commute, the time away from home with my husband, the harassment and culture I had now been putting up with for almost two years.

I looked up to find Stephanie, the VP of Marketing on my team, standing in my doorway. SHIT! My 2 p.m. meeting!

Stephanie, clearly oblivious to what had just occurred, stared at me curiously and politely asked if I was okay. "I'm fine," I stated, excusing myself for a moment under the pretense of needing to use the bathroom.

I rushed down the hall, praying for no encounters. Pushing open the door to the restroom, I headed for the handicapped stall because of its size and corner location. Leaning against the cool tile wall, I slid down into a squatted position (yes, while wearing five-inch heels) and started hyperventilating and full-on crying. I knew someone was waiting in my office. I had to pull my act together and be what I always was—a professional.

I grabbed a wad of toilet paper to wipe away the evidence. Emerging, the face in the mirror had mascara everywhere, blotchy skin, and red puffy eyes and nose. There was no hiding this.

I cleaned myself up as best I could, returning to my office with what I thought was stoicism. I somehow made it through the meeting. The VP clearly knew something had happened but was gracious enough not to inquire or acknowledge my state of being. I saw the concern in her eyes but was so grateful for how she handled it.

All I could think about was getting the hell out of there. My typical Thursday flight home was either at 4 p.m. or more often at 6 p.m., depending on the cost. Immediately

Chapter 35

after concluding my meeting, I called for an Uber and bolted to the airport. Over the years of doing this commute, I had the fortunate experience of regularly flying home with former Congressman John Lewis, as both of us did the same routine commute between Atlanta and DC. He always greeted me with a warm smile, called me "Blue Eyes" and we usually engaged in some banter. Today I hoped that I wouldn't see him. I wasn't up for conversation. I prayed that he wouldn't be on this flight to avoid him seeing me like this; luckily, God threw me a bone.

Because of my frequent travel with Delta, I usually got upgraded, and today was no exception. I threw my bag in the overhead and sank into 2A. The Fairy Godperson of flight attendants appeared, welcoming me, followed by, "Girl, I'm not even gonna ask if you want a drink because you look like you need one. (Ummm?... thank you, I think?) What can I get you?"

As I mentioned at the beginning of this story, I don't really drink. Occasionally, socially, when I do, I like champagne (actually, a lot!) or a good glass of red wine, but don't much care for the taste of hard liquor. I also learned the hard way many years ago on a girls' trip that alcohol and altitude are not a good combination for moi. Yes, guilty, I've used the bag in the back of the seat pocket.

Given the afternoon I'd just had, I thought I should make an exception.

"Vodka tonic. No, wait! Make it a double," I replied.

I grew numb as the flight progressed over the next hour. I stared out the window in disbelief, trying to process what had just happened. My body wanted me to cry, but I resisted the temptation.

During the flight and my Uber ride home, I repeated in my head over and over again how the situation unfolded.

I dreaded having to tell Bill. I was embarrassed. I got fired. I'd never lost a job before. I knew he would support and console me, but I cringed when I thought about how angry and frustrated he would be at my employer. We had both sacrificed so much for me to have this job. Notwithstanding the fact that he already hated my boss, this would send him over the edge.

The house was quiet and dark. Bill usually came home late on Thursdays; he'd pick up Mojo from doggie day camp and bring home dinner. I hadn't yet figured out how, when, or IF I was going to tell him. Obviously, it wasn't an IF; simply a matter of WHEN.

I kept obsessively reflecting on that afternoon's conversation, hearing the cold "I don't need you" over and over in my head, each repetition bringing forth a fresh wave of tears and nausea. Who treats people like that?

Chapter 36

"Be kind wherever possible. It is always possible."
Dalai Lama

As a senior executive and longtime manager of people, I have unfortunately been in the awful position on numerous occasions of having to relieve someone of their employment. It's never easy, but there is a right way and a wrong way to do it. In every case when I've had to terminate someone, it never came as a surprise to the employee. It was the last resort after coaching, counseling, and multiple warning shots had been offered; and it was always with cause. Termination for failure to perform had to always be well documented for legal reasons. I can still to this day recall detail-by-detail, three of the more difficult terminations I had to do during my career. Business is business, and that's your obligation, but I'm still a human, and taking away someone's livelihood, the way they support their family, is a horrible thing to have to do.

Even when a termination is warranted it is difficult, as was the case with one of my team members who was caught stealing . She was a single mom and full of hustle—she'd hustled me right into hiring her. Then we caught her stealing money, cashing payments sent in by check. She was a career criminal who, with a history of identity theft, had crept past our background process. The evidence was there;

she was cold busted. I had to walk her to a conference room where HR and law enforcement were waiting for her. She was arrested and left the building in handcuffs. I'll never forget her yelling at me as she was led out, "I'm a single mom! What am I supposed to do now?" The reality was, I felt bad for her—more so for her young daughter, whom I'd met. But people make their own decisions. She was a grown-up who knew right from wrong, and this was not her first rodeo. Still, that didn't make it easy.

The second one was about a year after I arrived at United Way. My predecessor had hired someone for a senior role shortly before her departure. He was not the candidate whom I would have hired, but he was there, and I was willing to give him a try. He couldn't do the job, and there were some personnel issues with how he treated his team. We talked multiple times at length, put together goals, tactics, and short, long-term improvement plans. Nevertheless, he still missed deadlines, didn't accomplish what he needed to, and his people were unhappy. We talked more; I tried different approaches. Nothing worked, and I was left with no alternative. He left me with no choice. Often, HR will do the termination, but in this case, while they were present, I needed him to hear from me why this was happening. Again, I felt terrible; he had relocated his family to take this job. But he couldn't DO the job, and as hard as I tried to change that for him, he wasn't willing to change it for himself.

The third and hardest one was also at United Way. It was a manager on my team, not my direct report. I liked this young man as a person; I respected him professionally. He'd often stop by after hours, and we'd talk; I got to know his backstory. An immigrant whose family had left their native country under political chaos, where he had also been

Chapter 36

studying to become a doctor. His father was a diplomat. They spoke no English when he arrived in his early twenties. And making matters worse, his father's health began to fail, and he was forced to quit the menial job he'd taken. He was the sole supporter of his parents. He also had a young son who lived out of state with the child's mother. This employee was bright, optimistic, and always brought ideas—good ones, too—to the table. But he messed up. Bad. As I said, the only real mistake is when someone dies. That's the one thing you can't fix. Anything else is simply a learning experience.

Unfortunately, one day he made a mistake that was hard to overlook—he lied. He cheated and stole, then tried to cover it up. He cried when I confronted him. His personal situation was dire, but that wasn't the reason for his actions. They were just simply, unfortunately, stupid. HR recommended he get nothing. The human in me ensured that he received a severance package.

In contrast to the difficult aspects of being a leader, there were also moments in the job that brought joy. For example, during my second year at United Way, when each of the top three performers on our respective teams was eligible for a minimal spot bonus. I also had thirteen additional people whom I felt had overperformed, and I bonused them right out of my pocket.

None of that ever happened to me—either the positives or the negatives. Well, except now for getting fired. Not only was there rarely any internal recognition or praise for the good work I had done, but I also received no coaching, no counseling, nor even an improvement plan that was presented to me prior to my termination, because *there was no issue with my performance*, or my integrity, or anything else. That's not to imply I'm perfect—none of us are, but there had been no documentation nor citing of issues that warranted this. Not a single discussion—ever—in my entire time of employment there.

And sadly, absent too were the little moments of joy where I felt appreciated and valued at United Way. This man, the soulless CEO, had never so much as wished me a happy birthday, even though they were published monthly; nor did he ever acknowledge years of service anniversaries. The exact manner in which he callously terminated my employment, and the underlying reason why, says so much about his constitution and character as a member of the human race.

Chapter 37

"You never know how strong you are until being strong is the only option."
Bob Marley

That night, as the scene played over and over in my head, I was lost. How would I explain to my husband, my dad, my friends, my professional colleagues that I had been FIRED while at the top of my game, for no other reason than the CEO had not bothered to accept an ounce of accountability for the toxic culture he had enabled? When my husband came home, thankfully, he was tired, and there was no conversation about my workday.

I was drained and went to bed early but never really slept; the TV was on, re-runs of *The Office* playing back-to-back into the early morning hours. The following morning, I contacted the COO via email, asking for a call to discuss my exit package. She informed me they hadn't put one together yet, the focus was on an announcement surrounding the arrival of the Chief Experience Officer the following week. I was instructed to just "be quiet and continue doing my job" until she could address this. REALLY??? Be quiet (like a good girl) and keep doing my job when I had just been fired? Was she fucking kidding me?

That day—TGIF—passed in a blur as I continued to "do my job," holding calls and meetings previously scheduled. My heart wasn't in it—how could it be—but I wasn't going to give anyone an opportunity. I would do my job to the same standards until the very last minute I was there. Whenever that might be.

When I thought things couldn't get any worse, they did—not surprising given how things had gone recently. However, first I needed to make it through the weekend and have the dreaded conversation with my husband. I couldn't get the words out. And when I finally did, my other half didn't believe me. Not like he thought I was joking; he was simply incredulous about what had actually happened. And angry. In fact, furious. He'd been to events with me and witnessed the actions and behavior of the CEO, who had never been friendly or respectful to him. Imagine you are at a work event with your boss, your spouse is there, and your boss is blatantly rude to your spouse.

Needless to say, the hub was not a fan, which had probably been exacerbated by an incident that occurred at the Superbowl the year prior. We were at a black-tie event, having cocktails and hors d'oeuvres, when the CEO's wife asked her husband to hold her handbag for a second as she navigated her drink and the plate in her hand. Being a "man's man" (as I'm sure he thought of himself), his response to her was, "give it to Lisa, I'm not holding that." Disregard for his senior female executive; rude to his wife, to me, and in front of my husband, who stated, "That's okay. I'll hold it for you," I'm certain that was not a moment which endeared him to my boss. All of that being said, the underlying anger was at all that had been given up, missed, and didn't happen. Why? Because I wasn't here. As discussed during negotiations when I first joined United Way, the original plan with my commute was that I would be in Alexandria "full-time" for the first six months or so to stabilize the team, then probably every other week. The reality was that once

I started the job, I realized that wasn't feasible. To do the job, I needed to be there, and the unspoken expectation was that I would be. So I did, with no resentment on my part. This was the job I wanted, and this was what it took to do it; I was committed. It did cause some extra stress at home, though, but still came with full support from my husband for something I was so passionate about. We navigated it and made it work—most of the time. Now though, he was full-on livid. He served in the Marine Corps, so I'll leave that to your imagination. I was expecting to hear every four-letter word and accompanying variations, but that day, I even think I heard new words come out of his mouth.

As I said, the worst was yet to come. To kick off the new year, the following week, we had our Executive Retreat—one of those most incredible events I've already described. While I was "fired," I was technically still there and was told to keep quiet. The COO also informed me when we spoke on the Friday before the retreat that I was expected to be present and participate. Awesome. I could build out that year's strategic plan that I would never help bring to fruition.

Part of the planning for that year was to figure out, and quickly, how to get on track with the lagging revenue metrics. Both the CEO and CFO viewed a proposed dues increase as the answer.

However, the reality of the weekly published dashboard reports indicated that it was *Harasshole* who wasn't performing. He was OFF target by MORE THAN SEVENTY PERCENT! His efforts to digitally transform the organization by selling the Salesforce platform were constantly missing the mark—and he was the Chief Strategy and Transformation Officer, responsible for transforming United Way. The transformation was not a part of my job description, either directly or indirectly. Even though I not only met but exceeded all my goals, in subsequent legal responses and documents, somehow this story would change; I, and I alone, had apparently failed to transform United Way. The world is a very messed up place. At least at United Way.

So here I was, having to attend the Executive Retreat—you can only imagine how much I dreaded attending this one even more than the previous ones. Were the other executive members aware of the situation? I was under the impression, based on my conversations with the COO, that the other executive team members had not been made aware of my termination. Lies, lies, lies.

We spent the first morning of the retreat discussing the Chief Experience Officer's role at length and making elaborate plans to welcome him. Yeah, that was fun! As if attending the retreat itself wasn't uncomfortable enough, the CEO sat next to me at the meeting around a square table. I couldn't look at him. I didn't want to be in his presence. I chugged coffee as a nervous distraction, purposely turning my chair slightly away from him so there could be no eye contact, leveraging every inch of space for maximum separation.

During the break, I went to the restroom, and the President of the U.S. division bolted up and followed me, hot on my heels as I pushed open the door. She grabbed my arm, "I don't know how you are even sitting here and participating in this as professionally as you are, knowing that you're leaving. I couldn't do it. Kudos."

WTF?!? She knew. Throughout the rest of the day, it became clear that everyone was aware, even though no formal announcement had been made. Talk about uncomfortable. Determined not to let anyone see me sweat, I somehow successfully completed my role of Best Actress in a Horrible Reality Show in pursuit of an Academy Award and flew to Orlando that Wednesday evening where I had committed several months ago to present at a conference. Oh, and I was being honored with an award. Yep—this week was going to be amazing.

My presentation was at 3 p.m. that Thursday. At 2:54, I received an email on my phone with a formal separation notification from the COO. Hands shaking, I stepped to the front of the room to present my content. I can honestly tell you I don't know how I managed to deliver it. I was rattled. Had they timed this deliberately? It certainly felt like they did; the conference agenda was available publicly. People in the meeting who later learned the details of what had transpired just before I presented have all sworn that I gave an excellent presentation. I think they were just being kind and generous.

Attending the networking event at the conference that evening was tortuous. I smiled bravely, continuing to play the role of CMO of the world's largest non-profit, a role that nobody else besides me knew I no longer held.

The day after my presentation, I decided to formally engage legal counsel; I had already spoken to an attorney the previous Friday following my conversation with the COO. It was also that day that the announcement went out about the CEO's "guy" joining United Way. And quietly buried in the bottom of the last paragraph was a small statement that I would be departing. I had been offered no insight that this was going to happen, nor had I even been given the courtesy of having my team hear it directly from me. They read it, just like me, buried in an internal announcement which subsequently went out to the global network of United Ways a few hours later. That evening, my phone began to blow up.

The former President of the U.S. Division, who had resigned last summer following the death of her husband, called. She was shocked, not only at what had happened but how it had been announced. She shared that part of the reason why she resigned, even after a lengthy bereavement leave and an attempted return to work, was precisely because of the CEO and how he had bullied her. A previous President of the U.S Division, who was also female and a woman of color, had also resigned about a year after I arrived. It was the same story: the CEO was a "horrible person" and had also bullied her.

Calls started coming in from around the United Way network, with shock and disbelief being the prevailing reactions. Yet despite the reactions that were being expressed to me, I was still expected—one week after the notification of losing my job—to offer a professional response (read between the lines, "lie") about the separation and state that it was simply a business decision on the part of the CEO. One by one, each conversation I had chipped away a piece of my soul. Yet, not ONE of these folks who expressed their bewilderment stood up for me or contacted the CEO to express anger or disappointment. Why? Because he had such a reputation for being dismissive, difficult, and an overall a-hole that it was just easier not to deal with him, that was the popular sentiment in the network. He was not well-liked or respected, but people didn't want the drama that came with crossing or questioning him. Leading an organization by instilling fear and intimidation among its staff is the easiest way to create a toxic workplace, which I now had the pleasure of experiencing.

As I said earlier, I had also been stripped of the dignity of speaking with my own team, who had already been notified via the internal communication that went out. While my

Chapter 37

termination may have been viewed as inconsequential, this was no small matter for my team, for whom I also now had to worry about since they were now going to be led by someone new without any advance notice or preparation.

The fact that both internal and external communications went out without my knowledge or visibility was troubling; I oversaw the communications team. In the past, such notifications did not come together in five minutes, which meant that those who reported to me had been given prior knowledge of my exit. My team knew, possibly before I did, that I was being let go. In particular, my former assistant had been tipped off in November. The timing suspiciously coincided with when I'd gone back to HR and when they had launched an "investigation," which was positioned as at the bequest of the CEO—the same investigation that they dragged their feet on when responding to me with the findings. I'd later learn the full pack of lies and twists on the truth that they provided in legal responses. By the way, that's called perjury and was clearly poor judgment on their part. Furthermore, my attorney later concluded that as I had not even been presented with exit papers—only a verbal dismissal told with no witnesses present that I was fired—that technically I was still employed. This was further evidence of the retaliation against me.

Chapter 38

"That which does not kill us makes us stronger."
Friedrich Nietzsche

The following week I spoke with the COO, and we determined that February 21, 2020, one month out, would be my last day of work. This conversation occurred a mere three business days after the COO had sent over the separation paperwork—three days during which the internal communications event took place, and I had engaged counsel. One of the first things she asked in that discussion was if I had signed the paperwork yet. Legally, I had twenty-one days to sign it. Placing an employee under pressure to sign a separation notice during the consideration period is also illegal.

In an abundance of professionalism, I offered to complete certain things, and that would set my successor up for success. Why, you may ask? Because that's how I operate. I hold myself to a standard which I feel is correct, and while I knew damn well from having witnessed previous departures of other staff how the CEO would immediately trash and lay blame on that person the minute they were out of sight, and that indeed he would do that to me as well, my actions would speak for themselves, and I'd give nobody an opportunity for criticism based on anything they had observed or heard from me while I was still there.

I completed my portion of my team's final year-end reviews and set them up for merit increases, as well as left a complete record of their performance for "the guy." We had major deliverables at Superbowl, which I committed to support. I was the only one with a relationship with the television networks and thus offered to go to New York and ensure we were set for the following year—the local United Way network counted on this coverage to drive their local donations. And by also doing this, it fell off "the guy's" plate so he wouldn't have to worry about it. My performance made it clear that I continued to do my job to the very end.

> Let's take five here. Please pay attention. This is important for people to understand, and nobody ever tells you this when you are in a situation such as this one.
>
> It is both overwhelming and terrifying to be fired, even for me, who *always* has a plan. You suddenly get forced to think about the short term. How will you pay your rent or mortgage without a paycheck? How will you feed your family? These are some of the most important considerations, but there are also other things to think about. Consider what you are giving up by signing a severance package that your employer has offered. The severance package may extend your pay for a bit while providing a lump sum settlement, but in exchange, you'll likely be required to release your employer from all claims.
>
> When your employer offers a severance or separation package, I implore you, please review the terms of the proposed agreement to see what you are potentially

Chapter 38

giving up; your right to work for a competitor, your right to bring a legal claim against the employer, or your right to file and receive unemployment compensation. This can be even more important to your financial future than the compensation offered by your employer in a severance agreement. It's key to think about all of these claims and how likely you want to/need to work for a competitor, how strong your potential case may be against your former employer, and whether you will need unemployment compensation to pay your bills.

Once you consider the whole severance package—including whatever financial incentives your employer may be offering and the claims that you are waiving—you have a decision to make. Weigh the pros and cons of signing the agreement and decide whether it is in your best interest. As I learned, this is an intensely personal decision and often depends in large part on the strength of any claims that you may be giving up, the amount of money offered in the severance package, your need for immediate financial resources, and other personal factors. If signing the severance claim is in your best interest, then you should do it. However, if you believe that it is not in your best interest, you can and should refuse to sign it. The law does not require your employer to offer you a severance package, and the law does not require you to sign it. Your employer cannot force you to sign a severance package; however, they can legally refuse to pay you any severance funds if you refuse to sign a release of claims.

Okay, so back to the story. My attorney now had the separation package, and I was counseled to "hang tight."

Within ten days of getting my separation offer, I was in Miami for our Superbowl events. I'm sure this sounds cool, 'fired and still gets to go to Superbowl'—I assure you it was not. Yes, getting to attend the Superbowl was a great mix of fun and work, but this year my heart simply wasn't in it. I was there physically, but it was impossible for me to be present and enjoy the moment. Being around my co-workers made me uneasy, and in addition to several of my team members being there, the President of the U.S Division was also in attendance.

She and I attended the Thursday night NFL Players' Association event which actually went fine. It was just the two of us, and she was borderline warm and friendly. There was champagne. I drank it. A lot of it. I wasn't celebrating, but it took the edge off. Then things fell off the cliff the following day.

The President of the U.S. Division and I were in an Uber headed over to our exhibit at the NFL Experience, the massive exposition of all things NFL, Superbowl, and football curated for the weekend. It was about a thirty-minute ride with traffic. Her phone rang, and she switched it to the ear opposite me to take the call, but not before I saw the number pop up on the screen—the CEO.

I heard him ask her if she had seen me, to which she replied, "Uh-huh, yes," and his response was, "I wish she'd just go already—she's being difficult." Okay. WHAT??? Difficult? I had had zero contact with him since sitting in the retreat two weeks ago. I maintained all work responsibilities and held my head high. Apparently, "difficult" was that I didn't make his life easy by simply not walking out the day he terminated me. Sorry, not sorry. I could not believe what I had just heard and how much her attitude cooled off for the remainder of the weekend after that call.

Chapter 38

The following week I returned to my office in Alexandria. On Wednesday, February 5, the COO slithered into my office with narrowed eyes and a serpentine smile plastered on her face to inquire where my separation paperwork was. I was shocked and dismayed at how drastically her character had just morphed before my eyes like a snake who had shed its skin. I knew this woman, or at least I thought I did. It was clear she had sold her soul to the CEO. Smiling back and remaining calm as my heart pounded in my chest, I reminded her that by law, I had twenty-one days which was the following day, and she'd have a response from my attorney before the end of the day. My attorney was working on our response and informed me they'd receive it by the deadline. I didn't know what the "response" would look like; I hadn't seen a draft or anything and wasn't sure what to expect. I received it for review and edited it at ten that evening. It was essentially a counteroffer. A very, very reasonable counteroffer to the unreasonable offer they had made me.

Thursday, February 6, started as a cold, blustery day with a threat of afternoon snow showers in DC. It matched my mood. I was restless for the rest of the night after editing the documents and returning them to my attorney.

United Way had scheduled an all-staff meeting that day for which they flew the CEO's "guy" up since he would be starting the following week. I did not attend. He was late in arriving. If I were him, I would have flown up the night before to ensure I was present and ready, but that was not my problem to worry about. Earlier that morning, the COO stopped by again, demanding that I give them a response and that I sign the separation notice. I told her my attorney would be sending it by the end of the day. Clearly, this was intimidation as its most apparent—straightforward harassment. Later that morning, I held a two-hour meeting with the new VP of Data I had hired (remember, I was told to turn us into a data-driven organization), during which I helped him prepare his first presentation to a group of local United Ways. I also spent the day preparing for my TV network meetings slated for Tuesday and Wednesday the following week as I began to finalize the countdown to the 21st, my last day of work.

As the entire office headed to the meeting to meet "Guy Wonder," the weather took a turn for the worse. In D.C., when it snows, the city shuts down. Growing up in Chicago, snow doesn't phase me, but D.C. doesn't handle it well. I knew there was a risk of my flight being delayed or even being canceled. And since it was Thursday, I went ahead and checked out of my hotel. I just wanted to be home. Sunday was my birthday, and my husband was leaving for an overseas business trip that day.

After looking at the radar and seeing what was headed our way, I decided to catch an earlier flight. With that, the day unraveled from there, and the proverbial shit hit the fan over the next few hours, setting the stage for a long-drawn-out battle.

I Ubered to Reagan International and settled in the SkyClub at about 1:30 p.m. While waiting for the 3 p.m. flight, which was now delayed until 3:22 p.m., I was forwarded my attorney's response to United Way's general counsel. At 4:10 p.m., my email was disabled. As I counseled earlier, you don't have to sign a separation offer or waive your rights. But understand what can happen if you don't. I didn't. At first, I thought something was wrong with my email. I still had reviews to complete for some of my team members; I'd also committed to going to New York

Chapter 38

the following week. Then, it slowly dawned on me, and I became infuriated. I had spent that morning ensuring United Way would be successful, yet the organization just tossed me away like yesterday's garbage.

I have not heard from anyone at United Way since that day.

Chapter 39

"All the people who knock me down only inspire me to do better."
Selena Gomez

The following morning, several of my direct reports shared with me via text that at 7 a.m., the VP of HR sent them a text message asking them to gather on a call at 8 a.m. where they were informed that "we had jointly decided that the prior day would be my last day of employment." The spider began to weave its web of lies.

At 9 a.m., a similar meeting was held with my entire team. Throughout the day, I was getting the play-by-play of what was happening from several of my trusted people. Apparently, someone on my team had questioned the VP of HR about what had happened; why was I suddenly gone when they understood I'd be there until late February? Some of them still had their performance reviews outstanding that we had scheduled but had not yet completed.

That my team had understood, and in fact, had even been informed that I would be working until February 21. The response again was, "we jointly decided yesterday was her last day; it was mutual." Another question was asked that since they had not had an opportunity to say goodbye (I had led this team for almost five years), if was it okay to contact me? The response from HR was that technically, they couldn't tell them not to, but also strongly implied they shouldn't, scaring people about what might happen if they did. HR then proceeded to have my team members clear my calendar and contact the TV networks to cancel the meetings for the next week, telling them, "She's suddenly no longer with us," which technically, I guess was true.

Stupid, stupid me. I extend trust on credit with people. I assumed that if I did the right thing and behaved professionally and appropriately during this process, they would, too. What was I thinking? These were the folks who had FIRED me for speaking up about sexual harassment. Who had illegally retaliated against me for reporting it, breaking a federal statute? And I thought they were going to play fair? I must have had my head up my ass far more than I had realized. I've never felt so taken advantage of in my life.

Information continued to make its way to me about what was transpiring. The COO and VP of HR had offered up multiple conflicting stories about the outcome of the "investigation" conducted in November after I'd raised issues again. My team was told by the VP of HR that "we met with Lisa and *Harasshole* separately, then the COO and CEO met with them both, but I was not a part of that meeting." The only factual statement there is that *she* wasn't a part of that meeting because that meeting actually **never happened.**

The COO told the same group that the CEO had met with *Harasshole* and me in an attempt to arrive at a reconciliation. Again, patently false. They couldn't even get their story straight, and people were beginning to see right through it. But my former team members were afraid—afraid for their jobs, their careers. After all, if this could happen to a C-level female, how much more at risk were they?

Chapter 39

Since I was supposed to work through the following week, I decided that I would give myself the grace of truly taking it off. I hadn't been able to take a true vacation while at United Way. Days went unused, and even when I was off, I was never really off. There was always "something," and the CEO had zero respect for personal time or any work/life balance. I'd get calls and emails on Sundays, in the evenings, and literally, almost every vacation came with some type of emergency crisis to which I had to respond. I recall sitting in a farmhouse in the Tuscan countryside dealing with Hurricanes Harvey, Irma, and Maria, or a Sunday afternoon being disrupted after the Bataclan shootings in Paris because "we shouldn't lose a good opportunity to capitalize on a tragedy." Yep, that's exactly what he said.

While I had good intentions to give myself a break, I also needed a plan. I knew I just couldn't sit around the house wallowing in pity. I am a survivor, not a victim. Human contact is where I get my electro-current. I would head to Starbucks each morning for a while to join that crowd of remote workers and find myself a new community.

I was also going to be hard core about working out. I love to bust a sweat. I had only been getting to my beloved gym here on Sundays because I was gone all week. While I joined a gym next to the office, I didn't know anyone there and didn't have "people" with whom I could work out.

I was even going to brush up on some foreign language skills; I love languages, learn them easily, and it would give me something to focus on.

I started making a list of people I needed to connect with, figuring out my narrative as I explained I was back in Atlanta and seeking my next opportunity. I surmised it might take me a good six months to land a commensurate role; my network in Atlanta was severely fractured, having not been here for nearly five years.

I was going to write. I had thought about writing a book before (not this one!), and this might be a time to take a crack at that. I know me—very well.

I set my plans in motion, and the week quickly filled up. I set up breakfast and lunch meetings almost every day to begin networking. I refined my story; "the travel had been killing me, I needed to be back in Atlanta, so I was going to do some consulting while looking for my next opportunity." It sounded good in my head, but would it make it out of my mouth?

That Tuesday evening, I attended a networking dinner in Atlanta with other local CMOs. Some I knew, some I didn't. When I arrived, I saw one of the principals who seemed delighted, albeit a bit surprised to see me. He asked how it was that I managed to be in town and available.

I felt my cheeks start to flush and my stomach flip. Smiling brightly (or so I thought), I took a big gulp of water and said, "Well, I have some exciting news (and the Oscar goes to. . .). I've left my role, and I'm looking for my next great adventure." The flicker of shock on his face was palpable. I'm certain he was aware that I was lying; he just didn't know why, and I'm sure he would have never guessed in a million years that I had been FIRED.

The new CMO of UPS was the guest speaker for the evening. I'd met Kevin before—this ought to be interesting. I blabbered through my storyline, grateful that he wasn't super invested or interested in really hearing what I had to say.

Fortunately, I made it through that dinner, which felt like a good practice run for my new social scene. Inside though,

Chapter 39

I felt like I was experiencing the five stages of grief, which started with denial. I could not believe this had happened. And then I was angry—really angry.

During my networking process, I unexpectedly received a call from a long-time friend, Jamie. His sister is a well-known fashion designer who hosts an annual summit to lift up and support women entrepreneurs. He suggested that I attend the event in New York the first week of March as it would be a good opportunity to network. I hesitated, not sure if I was up for it, but my husband encouraged me to go, reminding me how New York was always good for my soul. So I agreed; New York is and has always been my escape, and I knew that getting lost on the streets for a few days in the city would help clear my head.

I knew I had valuable skills and wanted to stay busy, so while I sought out my next big adventure, I developed "Marketing Mojo." I would be a consultant, sharing my knowledge of marketing, communications, and social impact with others. For a fee, of course.

I headed to New York the week of March 2, 2020. (On the plane, I watched "Bombshell" with Nicole Kidman, about Gretchen Carlson—If only I'd had a crystal ball.)

Whenever I am in New York, I always meet with "my sister from another mister," Angela. We've known each other for two decades and are cut from the same cloth. Our usual rendez-vous is to meet for excessively overpriced coffee at The Lambs Club on 44th and 6th where we often sight celebrities. Previously we've run into Mr. Wonderful from *Shark Tank*, and even Kevin Richardson from the Backstreet Boys. Guilty. I took a selfie with him. That night, Tina Chen Craig, aka The Bag Snob, a fashion influencer whom I followed religiously, was there. I was super happy that I was dressed to kill that day in a Burberry plaid trench and some high-heeled black boots.

We ordered our soy lattes and food while I caught Angela up to speed on what had just transpired with me. Like a good New Yorker, her reply was peppered with F-bombs. She was first and foremost shocked that I'd tolerated the situation as long as I had, and also commented on how stupid *Harasshole* was to think he could pull that with ME, of all people. Between mouthfuls of yogurt parfait with really overpriced out of season berries, she just kept shaking her head in disbelief.

In the midst of planning for my next big move there was, however, a small emerging wrinkle: the start of a flu-like illness called Covid. That first week in March 2020, cases were starting to pop up in the U.S., although none of us had any insight into what we were about to face. The New York event, which had about 600 attendees, continued as scheduled and acknowledged the growing concern for the virus; there was to be no hand-shaking; elbow bumps only. There was hand sanitizer everywhere.

Held at the Rose Theater in the Shoppes at Columbus Avenue, the day was filled with inspirational sessions and speakers. One of them would turn out to be prophetic for me in terms of what I had just dealt with, former Miss America Gretchen Carlson. In July 2016, Gretchen filed a lawsuit against then Fox News Chairman and CEO Roger Ailes, claiming sexual harassment. Subsequently, dozens of other women also stepped forward to accuse Ailes of harassment, and Ailes resigned under pressure. In September 2016, 21st Century Fox settled the lawsuit, and Gretchen received a public apology; she was one of the first high publicity cases of 2016's #MeToo movement and my hero. She stood up, she fought back, and she won. She lost

Chapter 39

a lot, too, though. NOW, I knew why I was here. And I was beyond excited to be in the presence of this woman.

I waited in line to enter the conference. The excitement was palpable in the air. I chatted with those around me and instantly felt my soul get lighter. The energy of those around me nourishes my soul. This past almost two years of isolation has about killed me.

The morning kicked off with model Halima Aden talking about her journey navigating the world of high fashion while sticking to her values of wearing her hijab. As the sessions continued, I found myself physically leaning forward in my chair, taking in as much as possible. I was beyond excited to be here and hanging on every word, copiously capturing as much as I was cold as I furiously scribbled notes. Between sessions, I was meeting with as many fellow attendees as I could. After all, we were all women with a common purpose. I just wasn't an entrepreneur like they were. YET.

Gretchen was scheduled to speak mid-afternoon. Before she finished, I bolted out of the theater and hovered outside the door I believed she would exit from. I wanted to speak with Gretchen and seek her counsel. Somehow, sadly, I missed her.

As the event wrapped, there was a reception with cocktails and snacks. I attended and did a fair amount of networking, getting more comfortable with my "consultant" pitch and handing out my cards. I'd come pretty far in the past two weeks if I do say so myself.

As the reception began to wrap, my phone rang. My attorney. My heart started pounding in my chest. What was happening? I found a quiet bench away from the crowd and took the call. We had received a letter from United Way's outside counsel, who represented their insurance carrier.

Most companies will carry insurance on claims like these. The outside firm, of course, stated they found no merit to my claims—that *Harasshole* and I just didn't have a good personal or professional working relationship. Hell, these days, almost nobody gets along. But was that a reason to fire me? NO. They also claimed to have "extensive evidence and documentation showing my poor performance record that resulted in my termination." They don't because it doesn't exist.

Their inability to manage the process in a professional manner represents an absolute failure on their part. Not only did I have copies of all of my performance reports, including one signed off by the CEO just six weeks before my termination, but I also had all of the handwritten notes that came at the holidays with the usual gift box of chocolates (doesn't take much thought there) acknowledging my good works and contributions. Why I saved those, I'll never know, because they meant nothing, but looking back now, they were worth something—evidence.

Sitting on that bench in New York, I began shaking with anger. My poor performance? Was there no end to the lies and deceit to which these people would go? And why? What were they, or rather, he, the CEO, protecting with *Harasshole*? The running joke inside was that *Harasshole* must have had pictures of the CEO with a random farm animal, and that's why his behavior was tolerated. I knew the truth and that there was no merit to their allegations, but it still shook me. I had a long conversation with my attorney sitting there on the bench that evening. When we hung up, I realized everyone was gone, and I was sitting there alone in the lobby of the theater.

That night, I took a chance and emailed Gretchen, never imagining in a million years she would respond. But she

Chapter 39

did. That same evening. I shared with her that I had been fired in retaliation for raising the issue of harassment and for not having fired another woman who complained. She immediately asked a few questions and offered to help. We set up a call for the following Monday. I could not believe that she responded to me.

We spoke that next week, and since then, Gretchen has leaned in and embraced me, guiding me, helping me. She is truly THAT woman who will give of herself and look out for another. I am immensely grateful to her.

In the middle of March, the world tilted left with the full onset of Covid-19. My schedule of lunches and breakfasts came to a grinding halt. I so clearly remember going to the gym on the morning of Monday, March 16, and by that afternoon, it was closed indefinitely, and classes moved online via Zoom.

Along with everyone else, I began to traverse the "new normal" that the pandemic defined for us, though mine came with a double whammy. As people started losing their jobs, I somehow didn't feel as bad. I was part of a community again. And we were all trying to figure it out.

I began offering to do thirty-minute consultations with small businesses on LinkedIn, trying to help them figure out how to survive in this strange new world. I worked with companies internationally, too. I had built a strong content strategy on LinkedIn, which gave me a way to stay relevant.

On April 2, I got a message via LinkedIn that floored me. It was from the global board chair of United Way. I last saw her at United Way's December 13 holiday party; the following day, we had a board meeting and installed her as the Global Board Chair of United Way Worldwide. She and I had always had a good relationship and I both liked and respected her. At least until that point. She asked me to contact her via email, which I did, telling her that I hoped she was well during these turbulent times, and I was simply following up on her request to contact her. This was her reply:

"Thank you, Lisa. I wondered whether you might have any ideas of using technology to stay in touch with anxious patients without spending hours advising on WhatsApp and without enacting a fair remuneration structure. Mobile money payments are about the extent of what is available here, conducted over the phone where funds are placed in trust until collected. I fear the current lockdown will be extended (sic) through to the end of April and want to keep or minimize staff coming to and from the clinic in person. Self-included if possible! Reading your post and knowing how smart you are, I figured I should ask you for your thoughts and ideas. Appreciate you taking the time to respond. Warm Regards, X."

Wait, what? Did this woman, the BOARD CHAIR and the CEO's boss, not know I had been fired? Or even more confusing, if I was being fired for being incompetent, why would she be coming to me with this tech question? Or did she simply have the audacity to reach out to me thinking I was cool with what had happened and would be willing to help anyway?

I'm choosing to assume that she had not been told the truth about what had happened—yet another sign of how broken things were internally within the company.

I responded, telling her that I was happy to have a conversation with her. It just wasn't going to be the one she thought we would have, that's for certain. Thereafter, she went radio silent.

Chapter 40

"They tried to bury us; they did not know we were the seeds."
Mexican Proverb

Spring turned to summer; Gretchen and I kept in touch. My case had been at a standstill, but the woman I was instructed to fire (and refused to do so) had also filed a claim with the EEOC. After my departure, they began making things very rough for her at United Way, essentially having her do my job without the title or the pay. Wasn't the CEO's "guy" the new marketing genius? According to my former team, it turns out he didn't know jack shit about marketing and dumped it all on this woman.

In late June or July, I asked Gretchen her opinion on going to the media with my story. After all, United Way received donations from nearly EIGHT MILLION people[1] and solicited the employees of more than half of the Fortune 500[2]. Didn't the donors have a right to know what was going on at the organization so they could make an intelligent choice about where to allocate their money? If I spoke up and shared what had happened to me, would anyone else dealing with the same issue also be inspired to do so? And if the answer were yes, then speaking out would be worth it if

---

[1] 2019 United Way Annual Report.
[2] https://www.unitedway.org/doing-good.

just one other person was helped by it. I wanted Gretchen's opinion on whether this was even a newsworthy story that anyone would want to cover. She felt it was and offered up four reporters for me to contact. Two were with national publications, one was with a women's magazine, and the fourth was more in the political sphere.

Before considering to interview me, they all requested to see my EEOC filing and documentation on what had transpired. With permission from my attorney, they received a version with names redacted. Three of the four were interested. The fourth, who is at a well-known national newspaper, told me that she didn't see allegations of sexual assault, so what exactly was my complaint? Sexual harassment is not simply a physical issue. Verbal interactions are well within the bounds of harassment. Apparently, without a horrifying physical encounter that would have caused me even more damage, to this reporter, a female no less, it simply wasn't salacious enough for her to cover.

I'll never forget her or how I felt at that moment. Women often do a poor job of sticking together. I vetted those reporters just as much as they were trying to suss a story out of me. In the end, there was one reporter with whom I felt comfortable and who had extensive experience covering topics of this nature: Emily Peck at *HuffPost*.

Emily and I began talking in August of 2020. I respected the fact that she wasn't going to write "my story" but rather was going to write "the story." She's an investigative journalist and researched facts, solicited outside opinions, etc..., and created the narrative from her vantage point.

While providing her documentation on my case, I tripped across something that sent flashbulbs off in my head. A VP of Labor Relations at United Way, Ana Avendano, had been terminated in March of 2019. The reason given to the executive team in an email from the COO was that it was related to bullying about something she posted on LinkedIn at the time of termination. Her posting was tied to allegations of sexual harassment within the United Way network that Ana had raised on behalf of other women. Ana had uncovered sexual harassment in the local United Way network; local labor leaders were propositioning and groping female United Way workers hired to coordinate union fundraising. When these women spoke up about mistreatment to their local United Way leadership, their complaints were ignored, or worse, they faced retaliation. Ana took on the issue and became an advocate for these women, declaring to them that they should not have to put up with this behavior.

In 2016, before *Harasshole* was there and my issues even started, Ana was already dealing with the issue locally.

Sarah, a local United Way employee in the Midwest, reached out to Ana and told her that at fundraising events where there was alcohol, she had been groped and propositioned by a local United Way board member repeatedly over the years. He was also a member of the union (part of the AFL-CIO network) in her community.

When Sarah complained about harassment in the past, the local union leadership offered no help, essentially telling her to deal with it herself. She kept quiet until the fall of 2016. At a Halloween fundraising event, the board member who had been harassing her paid a waitress $20 so he could "motorboat" (place his mouth between her breasts and blow) her. The incident, which many saw, caused a stir.

When the local leaders at United Way asked Sarah about it, she revealed that this man had harassed her for years. Her local United Way said it was obligated to investigate her claim that he had harassed her. And even though she asked to keep her name private, the local branch didn't respect that.

This was the start of Sarah's nightmare. When word spread that she'd reported the board member, backlash from her fellow union members and her local United Way was swift. She ran into a fellow union member, who "walked by and whispered in her ear, 'f*cking c*nt.'" Now, if this isn't retaliatory, I don't know what is. I spoke to Sarah about the *Huffington Post* investigative report; Sarah then spoke to Emily.

This is the environment that we, as professional women, were living in. All we wanted was to go to work, do our jobs, and be respected by our male colleagues for our contributions and value. We were not there to get complimented for our appearance, to be objectified, and certainly NOT there to face retaliation when we raised the issue, which we were obligated to do by written policy.

Chapter 41

"You must be the change you want to see in the world."
Mahatma Gandhi

This is a critical point; almost every organization has policies and training that govern sexual harassment and inappropriate behavior in the workplace. If they're not actionable, they may as well not exist. Most policies place an obligation on employees to report even suspected cases of bad behavior. Our policy explicitly stated that failure to notify HR could result in termination. I think they had it wrong; notifying HR *will* result in termination.

Unfortunately, and apologies for the political commentary, but since 2016 and the election of Donald Trump, we have been living in a society where there is more and more normalization of bad behavior and less and less consequence for those that perpetuate it. When people see behavior that is wrong, and there is no accountability for it, it becomes normalized—they think it's okay.

If you were at a restaurant and saw a table next to you perform the infamous dine and dash, you'd think that's not okay, right? But what if the table next to them did it too because they realized that nobody had chased the other folks down. And then a third table did it; maybe you'd start to think it was acceptable behavior. That is what happens when there's no accountability, no consequences for behavior outside our societal norms.

Corporate America, unfortunately, in recent years has made a consistent practice of dismissing bad behavior. They really should do better. Let me say it louder for the people in the back: HEY FOLKS, CLEAN UP YOUR ACT. DO BETTER. Even in recent weeks as I have been writing this book, Andrew Cuomo, Governor of New York, begrudgingly resigned after a truly independent investigation found merit to the claim that he had harassed at least eleven women. The new host of *Jeopardy!* Mike Roberts stepped down after only a single day of taping when a history of sexist remarks and a discrimination lawsuit emerged. And right as we were going to press, my beloved "Mr. Big" from *Sex and the City*, Chris Noth, was accused of sexual assault by two women. I'm crushed.

Although still totally unacceptable, I can understand the evolution of bad behavior in Corporate America and how it has become normalized. The entertainment sector, too, has long had this as part of its culture with the infamous "casting couch." The name Harvey Weinstein is itself enough to evoke how engrained such despicable behavior is in this industry. And politics, with its trappings of power, sure; take Matt Gaetz, who is being investigated for sex trafficking of a minor as a prime example.

United Way certainly had its own sordid scandal in the past. The former CEO, William Aramony, was ultimately indicted on criminal charges of fraud and financial mismanagement in 1995 and served prison time. Concurrent with that, there were several allegations of inappropriate sexual behavior, including with underage girls and two sisters, one of whom was seventeen and pursued by the then fifty-nine-year-old Aramony. There was outrage from the United Way network, and many of the locals withheld paying dues to the national office in protest. In 1992, during the "scandal," he announced his "retirement"—with full benefits, by the way—it's all there on Wikipedia. History certainly has a way of repeating itself.

The non-profit sector is not immune to this behavior. It's simply that people are hesitant to speak up, not necessarily out of fear, but out of reluctance to harm the mission itself. This came out loud and clear in some of the media interviews with former employees who themselves had experienced or witnessed the same behavior I did under the same leadership, but kept quiet because they didn't want to harm United Way. They suffered in silence or voluntarily left roles which they were good at or truly committed to rather than harming the organization.

Honestly, I had a small bit of that internal battle myself. I knew that donors regarded United Way as one large entity and didn't discern between United Way of "Anytown" and United Way Worldwide. The locals would potentially pay the price for my speaking out when they had nothing to do with it. In the end, I had to reconcile this in myself and speak my truth.

United Way, who stated by virtue of the marketing campaigns which I had created, that they fought for every person in every community. However, they certainly didn't fight for us; they fought against us for calling out their bad behavior, and there needed to be some accountability for what we had endured.

Chapter 42

"The secret to change is to focus all of your energy not on fighting the old, but on building the new."
Socrates

Let's return to Sarah's story. In 2017, when the man was finally kicked off the local United Way board, it was too late for Sarah, who finally felt she had no other choice than to leave her job.

Richard Trumka, the head of the AFL-CIO with whom United Way had a long-standing relationship, complained to the CEO about Ana raising the visibility of these issues. She, too, had filed a complaint with the EEOC, claiming she was subjected to both a discriminatory and retaliatory environment.

It took Ana and me a while to connect since she had blocked all of the United Way executives from her LinkedIn page, which was the only way I had to reach her. As you've likely learned by now, when challenged, I'll find a way. And I did.

Ana and I had a friend in common, and I was sure she had confided in her. I was right. She had copies of all of Ana's legal documents and was able to provide them to me.

Ana had settled her case with United Way about six weeks prior, and fortunately, her confidentiality agreement with the organization allowed her some limited ability to discuss broad systemic issues. And now, along with Sarah, she too agreed to speak with Emily at the *Huffington Post*. Our story was gaining strength and continued to grow; the woman who filed the third EEOC suit, the one whom I was told to fire when she, too, complained about *Harasshole*, agreed to talk to Emily as well. Three EEOC charges were filed within a single year by three females, two of whom were women of color. Where there is smoke, there is fire.

Emily and I would check in regularly so that I could update her with what I was learning or so that she could clarify any questions she had for me. And to make an even stronger case, in addition to the three of us who had filed official complaints, Emily also spoke with six former employees, who provided her with more details about how the organization treated women.

It had been six months since I had filed, and I still had heard nothing from the EEOC. Nagging me in the back of my head, still, too, was the LinkedIn and email exchange I'd had with the Chairwoman of the Board of Directors. What exactly had they been told? I'm sure it was something not true, performance-related, and that was defamatory. I've held multiple seats on boards as I do currently. The obligation of a Board of Directors is to the organization, not the CEO.

Wouldn't members of the two United Way Boards want to know what happened? Especially those who had committed their time and talent to the organization's progress, surely, they would want to address this.

After consulting my attorney, I drafted a letter to the boards in October. There were two boards of directors: a U.S. board and a worldwide board. The CEO was accountable to the Chair of the worldwide board. Sitting on those boards was a veritable "Who's Who" of Corporate America: C-level executives from Deloitte, U.S. Bank, Whirlpool, Nationwide

Chapter 42

Insurance, and Wells Fargo. I think you get the picture. High-level executives whose own organizations had policies governing this type of behavior. With their organizations publicly affiliated with United Way, I was certain they'd be aghast and want to protect the reputation of their own companies as well.

I felt confident that writing to the boards would be an effective strategy that would result in successfully resolving this. I still believed deep down in the promise of United Way and the work they did, notwithstanding the CEO and *Harasshole's* behavior. All I ever really wanted, aside from never having had this happen at all, was a reasonable settlement and someone to acknowledge and address what was happening there. It goes back to my theory about extending credit on trust. I thought that given the opportunity to do the right thing, people would. That was then—I'm now pretty jaded on that.

On October 14, 2020, I sent the following letter to the Boards.

> Dear Members of the United Way Worldwide and U.S. Boards,
>
> With a heavy heart, I write to you in confidence to make you aware of disturbing behavior that I was subjected to and witnessed during my time at United Way – in the hopes that you will take actions to address these problems.
>
> Under [CEO], United Way suffers from a toxic culture, where sexual harassment and other abusive behaviors are not only tolerated, they are actively covered up—and employees who follow policy by reporting it often face retaliation.
>
> As many of you were likely told, my position was "eliminated" in January 2020 to make room for a Chief

Experience Officer. That is not the whole story, and I believe the Board has a right to know the truth.

On March 17, 2020, I filed a complaint with the U.S. Equal Employment Opportunity Commission, the federal agency that administers and enforces civil rights laws against workplace discrimination, harassment, and retaliation, alleging harassment and retaliation for reporting sexual harassment to our Human Resources department, pursuant to United Way policy.

Please note: EEOC charges are filed under penalty of perjury.

After enduring inappropriate behavior by a fellow member of the senior executive team for a period of approximately 15 months, I finally reported him to HR in February of 2019. A few weeks after that and throughout 2019, I subsequently endured a systemic pattern of retaliation from [CEO], which culminated in my termination in January of this year. Here are a just few of the more salient points from my filing:

- In February 2019, a junior administrative employee told me and one of my direct reports (a female VP who was her supervisor) about her experience of potential sexual harassment by the same perpetrator, including inappropriate comments and unwanted attention at an after-hours event sponsored by United Way. As directed by employee policy, we both alerted HR.
- In March 2019, after receiving an affirmative response from [CEO] that he was aware that I had had to go to HR to report this behavior, [CEO] told me: "You are going to have to learn to get along with [the perpetrator]."

Chapter 42

- Also, in March, [CEO] directed me for the first of three times to terminate the female VP who also went to HR on behalf of her subordinate. This individual had consistently been a top performer and there was no legitimate justification for her termination, so I refused.
- In April 2019, during an annual performance review, [CEO] began demonstrating a change in attitude toward me. For the first time in three years, he began giving downgraded feedback on my performance.
- In the months that followed, [CEO] began pulling resources away from my team and allocating them to the perpetrator's team. I was not allowed to backfill these resources, yet also was not relieved of the work.
- In December, [CEO] announced plans to hire a new position, a Chief Experience Officer, that would aggregate all customer facing work, including the teams led by the perpetrator and me.
- In January of this year, [CEO] called me into his office and told me: "...I don't need you" and to "get with [the COO] and work out the details."

I firmly believe my termination was a direct result of the reports of sexual harassment I made to HR. What's more, I understand that mine is just one of several EEOC charges filed against United Way Worldwide since March 2019 by female employees who also faced discrimination, harassment, and retaliation, including termination, for reporting sexual harassment and other inappropriate behaviors. In contrast, the perpetrators of sexual harassment in the workplace have been protected or, in some cases, promoted.

Please know that it was not an easy decision for me to come forward with my story, but I simply could not continue to remain silent. To do so makes me also complicit. I am speaking out on behalf of all of those other employees who are too afraid or intimidated to do so.

Like me, I truly believe that all of you became involved in United Way for good reasons, based in a desire to improve your communities by serving others in need.

Unfortunately, [CEO's] leadership at United Way is jeopardizing those noble goals and putting your reputations—and the reputations of the companies you represent—at risk.

I urge you to take action to address these issues. I remain available to assist in any way I can.

With respect,
Lisa Bowman

The next morning, I received the following:

Dear Ms. Bowman,

I hereby acknowledge receipt of your letter dated 14 October 2020.

Be assured that the contents will be addressed and responded to with the utmost gravity and expedience.

Yours sincerely,
[Board Chair]

That was all I ever heard from the board. At least I knew where I stood. Didn't they realize that the organizations for whom they worked were now potentially at risk via their affiliation with United Way?

Chapter 43

"It took me quite a long time to develop a voice, and now that I have it, I am not going to be silent."
Madeleine Albright

In early November, United Way contacted my attorney with a settlement offer. It was still unacceptable. Now, before you go and think this was all about money for me, while I can't legally disclose settlement details, I can tell you that given all that had happened, their settlement proposal, which only represented several weeks of salary, did not include the bonus I had earned for the prior year, and did not even cover the legal fees I had incurred because of United Way's lack of accountability. This was not going to cut it. Trust me, if you were walking in my heels, none of you would have taken this offer either, particularly when it was accompanied by a "shut your mouth" clause.

While my husband was worried about my going public because of haters and trolls, the opposite happened. People came out and rallied in support. Even people who were still working at United Way offered me their encouragement, discretely and quietly.

What is most frustrating about this situation was that had HR and the CEO responded to me in a manner that was sincere and respectful, the shitshow that followed may have never happened. My lawyer had even given them a courtesy heads-up that I was receiving counsel from Gretchen and was likely to go to the media; their counsel dismissed it, practically laughing in my attorney's face.

I think it is safe to assume that United Way started to realize this was going to go public when Emily contacted them for a statement before finalizing the article. The Friday before Thanksgiving, they dropped a note to the network letting them know there "might be some media coverage the following week," failing to disclose its nature or to provide speaking points to the locals. Bad plan. It left the local United Ways on their own to fend for themselves. And they were not happy.

On Saturday, November 21, I learned that Emily's piece was going to press on Monday. At the last minute, I asked Emily to redact *Harasshole's* name from the article. I knew he was unstable from his demonstrated behavior, and I was worried not only about my personal safety but about the potential for him to go over the edge after being outed and perhaps harm himself. Call me selfish, but I didn't want that on me. Truth be told, he was only the catalyst for this situation; my real issue was with the CEO and his failure to address it instead of placing that onus on me.

I also had another "to-do," which I was dreading with everything in my soul. Telling my dad. I didn't even tell him that I had lost my job until April or May. We never really even talked about it; I think he assumed it was a Covid related layoff, and I didn't correct him. I couldn't get the words out. It was still raw. But with national press coming, I had to.

I usually talk to my dad on Sunday afternoons. That Sunday, I started stressing around mid-day, my head filling with dread in anticipation of the conversation. It had to be done; I procrastinated as long as I could, then pushed the "Dad" button on my phone, grinding my teeth with each

Chapter 43

ring. My stomach was in knots. I remember sitting on the floor in the master bath, leaning up against the cool glass of the shower. Odd place to make a call, I know, but it was close to the tissues which I knew I'd need.

Our usual Sunday chat began by discussing his golf score, Covid, and world events. As we brought the conversation to its natural end, I said, "Hey, by the way, there's something I need to tell you." The rest of it was delivered between tears, long silent pauses, and gasps for air as I began hyperventilating from crying so hard. I honestly couldn't tell you the specifics of the conversation as I was so emotional. I somehow felt like *I* was confessing to having done something wrong. Victim-shaming—when we are made to feel that we have somehow brought this upon ourselves. To be clear, that's not how he made me feel. But he is a bit older and was in the workplace during an era when #MeToo didn't exist. He was supportive, and when we hung up, I was drained. I had to re-charge my batteries for what was to come the next day. Tom Hanks and Meg Ryan were *Sleepless in Seattle*; I was *Sleepless in Atlanta*.

Chapter 44

"If you are neutral in situations of injustice, you have chosen the side of the oppressor."
Desmond Tutu

As Thanksgiving week began, the next morning, Monday, November 23 at 5 a.m. to be exact, the following headline appeared in the *HuffPost*:

> *United Way Accused of Retaliation Against Women Employees*[3]

Three women filed federal charges against United Way Worldwide, accusing CEO Brian Gallagher of targeting them after they spoke up about sexual harassment. Two were fired.

The 6,000-word article by Emily Peck laid out what had happened to me, Ana, Sarah, and another woman who was kept anonymous at her request. It detailed the harassment, the bullying, and the toxic culture at United Way. It also covered the former scandal.

Emily cited quotes from six former United Way employees about how the non-profit treats women. All asked for anonymity, fearing career fallout, and citing United Way's outsized influence in the non-profit

---

[3] https://www.huffpost.com/entry/united-way-retaliation-female-employees_n_5fb82c61c5b67493dd366529

community. Each one of them also emphasized the importance of the non-profit's work and mission.

They were hesitant to publicly criticize an organization that does so much good but added that it is precisely this reticence that allows harassment and misconduct to flourish unchecked. "Within the United Way [network], we're all cautious because we don't want to harm the brand that helps people," said one former employee. "So, people have kept their mouths shut. We don't want to cause problems for the mission."

Within hours of the article dropping, I was bombarded with messages and calls. As Emily, Gretchen, and I had independently promoted the article on social media channels, the phone kept ringing, my inbox filling up with emails, text messages were pouring in, and even my LinkedIn messages were exploding.

The outpouring of support was the only thing that held me vertical that day. I received messages from former United Way employees thanking me for speaking up on behalf of those who had been silenced. Some UPSers even told me they'd no longer give to United Way. Others from my past reached out to tell me how brave I was, how sorry they were for what I had gone through. Then there were the few who, even though we hadn't spoken in years, wanted all the salacious details.

At some point during the day, when I stopped to breathe for a minute and come down from the adrenaline high to assess my emotional state, I realized the fear had disappeared, and I felt strong—really strong. The decision to expose this organization's awful behavior was the right thing to do. Not out of spite or vengeance. I knew that I wasn't the only one. As long as *Harasshole* and the CEO were still there, others were at risk, given the long history behind

Chapter 44

the CEO's endorsement of bad behavior that wasn't endemic to just my situation.

The following day, I crashed. Mid-morning, while on a call, I suddenly felt super sick. So sick, I had to end the call. I never get sick, but by 10:30 a.m., I was back in bed with a sweatshirt on, two blankets, and my teeth chattering so bad I was afraid they'd shatter into pieces. I needed to get better and fast—I had another media interview that afternoon with *Business Insider*, who was also interested in covering the story.

I popped some Tylenol and took a quick power nap. No luck. At 2 p.m., when the reporter called, I was still pretty out of it. Speaking with her took every single ounce of energy left in my body, and I fell back asleep right after we hung up. I went for a COVID test that evening, scared and certain that I had somehow caught COVID and had to fight that battle in addition to all the others I was dealing with. Luckily, I didn't.

The following week I received a text message from someone I didn't know who tracked me down through three layers of mutual contacts. She wanted to talk. This woman had worked with *Harasshole* at a consulting company fifteen years prior. She had also had issues with him. While *Harasshole* was never named publicly in the *HuffPost* article, this woman knew that he had ended up at United Way, and she immediately knew it was him when she read the article. She also shared with me that he was ultimately terminated from that employer for similar inappropriate behavior.

She was the first of several from his past to contact me. Two women I had never met before, who had worked at his former local United Way, both shared with me their horror stories. I had suspected, but now knew beyond the shadow of a doubt that he was, in fact, a serial *Harasshole*. His behavior towards me wasn't random. Speaking with these women, they sounded strong-willed, good at what they did, and probably completely intimidated him. His insecurities were at the core of this as he struggled to exert power over those whom he felt may be a threat to his fragile ego.

Chapter 45

"You have to believe in yourself when no one else does."
Serena Williams

As the end of the year approached, I still hadn't heard anything from the EEOC. It had been nine months since I had filed my charges and yet no progress. I called the EEOC in early December; I was on hold for over two hours before I spoke with a human. The baritone voice on-hold message, permanently ingrained in my long-term memory, said, "Thank you for contacting the EEOC. Your call is very important to us."

The person who answered my call provided me with a name for the lead investigator on my case, a phone number, and an email—WOO-HOO! On Friday, December 4, I had my first interaction with my EEOC investigator, who helped me understand what had been happening. United Way's counsel had requested extensions on the paperwork they owed the EEOC in response to my filing. The last contact had stated they would provide it on October 23, which they failed to do.

By the end of that day, after much back and forth, I learned that the EEOC investigator provided United Way's attorney a new deadline of Monday, December 7, to respond, which had originally been due in May.

On Tuesday, we received the response which United Way had filed that Monday. Legally, I can't share its contents, but I can tell you it was weak at best. It was essentially a handful of pages of what they perceived, in my estimation, to be "substantive content" bookended by all of the policies they had in place. Further, it also included an attempt to lay blame for the organization's poor employee engagement score at my feet. The response alleged poor performance on my part and acknowledged that I had failed to get along with and create a positive working relationship with *Harasshole*. In short, not only did it contain several inaccuracies but also some outright lies.

We had until December 28, 2020, to provide a rebuttal to the EEOC. My attorney and I worked closely on it and submitted a narrative of events and our supporting exhibits. While the EEOC doesn't adjudicate, they can issue someone who has filed charges against an employer the "Right to Sue." There are essentially two positive dispositions that can be obtained here, a "Right to Sue" and a "Determination of Cause with a Right to Sue." The latter is when upon examination of the artifacts submitted by both parties, the lead investigator determines that the charging party has probable cause to sue. If the investigator reaches this conclusion, then the charge escalates to the District Director for approval. Once s/he approves it, the Letter of Determination is sent to both parties, and an invitation to conciliate is offered to the employer. If both parties are willing, the EEOC will mediate and help negotiate the terms of the settlement. If the offer is denied, the EEOC determines whether or not it wants to litigate the case itself. This only happens in a very small percentage of cases. If they do not litigate, a Right to Sue (Conciliation Failure) is issued to the Charging Party.

Chapter 45

Spoiler Alert, but please finish reading until the end and finish the book: at the time of publication, the EEOC has still not yet issued a ruling. Nonetheless, I am optimistic I will receive a Determination of Cause. The EEOC will ask United Way if they'd like to attempt a "conciliation," and if they refuse, I will sue them. They stole my career, my financial stability, and my emotional well-being.

On December 23, 2020, the *Business Insider* article, written by Yelena Dzhanova, was published. While she was a little more hard-hitting than Emily's article, it wasn't any better or worse, just a different style of coverage. Yelena's headline read, "United Way... Has A History of Rewarding People Who Engaged in Sexist Behavior."[4] Her story shared the perspectives of nine former employees and covered items that *HuffPost* did not: allegations that the exclusion of female employees is facilitated by the organization's women-run HR department and that women of color, in particular, had been dismissed and treated as "inconveniences" despite their advanced degrees and being well-respected in their fields. *Business Insider* also stated that "for decades, misogyny has been rampant across the organization's leadership, according to detailed accounts from nine former United Way workers employed at the organization from the early 1990s to the beginning of 2020."

Once again, I felt vindicated; this wasn't an isolated incident—it wasn't just me—and I didn't imagine it. This went far beyond *Harasshole* and was a scathing indictment of the CEO and the incidents that had occurred for years under his leadership.

---

[4] https://www.businessinsider.com/united-way-rewarded-men-accused-of-sexism-former-employees-say-2020-12

There were tales of long-standing inappropriate behavior by the former COO (*Mr. Hand-sy*), who had a thirty-year plus personal relationship with the CEO who was aware of the allegations but hired him into a national role anyway.

A CEO from a local United Way in Ohio had resigned in February 2016, according to an organization press release which at the time stated that he left to "pursue other opportunities." One former employee said he had resigned after he was accused of sexual misconduct with a subordinate. *Business Insider* sourced a February 2016 story from the Ohio newspaper *Cleveland Scene* saying that he "had been permitted to quietly resign after his behavior involving a subordinate employee became impossible to ignore." Four months later, he was hired as a consultant by the CEO at United Way Worldwide. I did my own checking on this, speaking to a former employee who absolutely would have known if the CEO was aware of this, and was told emphatically, "Yes, he knew and didn't care about it at all."

I laughed cynically at the Board's response to this article, "that it was 'deeply disturbed by any allegations of misconduct and pledges to eradicate such behavior from our organization."

Really???

The article further cited that the board stated that it had "authorized an independent third-party investigation of the process by which certain allegations were handled, all relevant policies and procedures, and an assessment of the corporate culture that might have fostered any such conduct." It's unclear whether this investigation would involve talking to any former employees. Spoiler alert! It didn't.

Chapter 45

There were horror stories about women being referred to as MILFs and being passed over for promotion because they were pregnant. The article also cited Stacey Stewart, the former President of the U.S. Division for United Way Worldwide, being told by the Public Relations team to "make sure she doesn't outshine [the CEO]."

No doubt, the article in *Business Insider* was very damning.

Chapter 46

"If you don't risk anything, you risk even more."
Erica Jong

On December 22, 2020, a group of roughly twenty former female United Way Worldwide employees sent a letter to the United Way Board of Directors stating that, "Our purpose in writing this letter is to share that the experiences voiced by the women on November 23, 2020, *Huffington Post* article are not surprising nor unique. Each of us has either witnessed, experienced, or been made aware of various levels of discrimination, harassment, and/or retaliation for reporting such issues while employed at UWW. . . . Our collective time at UWW spans more than two decades, and this culture was in place during our tenure. While we had many accomplishments during our time at United Way, we believe we could have been much more effective if we had not been mired in and distracted by these circumstances. . . ."[5]

The same women surveyed former female employees and shared the results with the board.

- 96% of survey respondents strongly agreed or agreed with the attached letter, 4% were neutral.
- No survey respondent agreed that women had equal opportunities as men to advance professionally at UWW.

---
[5] https://www.scribd.com/document/489980504/Letter-to-UWW-Board-Chairs#from_embed .

- 84% of survey respondents responded that they personally experienced at least one of the following while working at UWW: harassment, discrimination, or pay equity issues.
- Of the respondents who shared they reported the above issues to Human Resources or management, all of them answered NO when asked, "Were actions taken to assure you that there was zero tolerance for misconduct?" as indicated in UWW's official response to the Huff Post article.
- 91% of survey respondents do not believe it is possible to create a healthy work environment for women at UWW with the current top leadership in place.

I believe this letter was written entirely in good faith. First and foremost, I was unaware of it and only knew two of the women involved, as I had come to realize after the letter was released. And I didn't know either of them well; we hadn't crossed paths during my time at Worldwide and only knew each other in passing from when I was at the Foundation at UPS. Second, the letter was well-written with data to back it up. It was respectful and offered tangible solutions so that United Way would be sustainable for the future. It goes back to what I said about people not wanting to come forward because of the potential of damaging an organization that existed to do good. They even offered to meet with the Board to help them craft a direction forward.

Two days later, on December 24, the board sent an unengaged response that showed just how inept they were. In large part, it stated:

> "Let us first speak directly to the questions you raise concerning our commitment to female employees

and to your experiences at United Way. As members of this organization, we are familiar with the unique challenges many of our female employees face in their careers and obligations to family, friends, and communities—especially this year. Their personal success requires not just personal courage but organizational support. Together you, along with numerous others, exemplify the former; it is the Board's commitment to you, and one we are undertaking, to ensure the latter is cultivated.

We know more can be done, but we firmly believe we have made significant progress to date. UWW is committed to supporting women in the workplace and recently engaged an outside firm to conduct a comprehensive assessment of our compensation levels, which determined that women and men were paid equally for the same positions.
Additionally:

- 69% of UWW directors are women; 48% of VPs and above are women.
- Between 2019-2020, 74% of promotions were earned by female employees, and, of that number, 50% were promotions to Director level or higher roles.
- United Way also prides itself on offering flexible work arrangements for its staff, including flexible work hours, compressed work schedule, four hours of paid administrative leave per week, telecommute, and temporary telecommute options."

Honestly, their response had nothing to do with what was raised in the letter. They couched it all under the issues COVID had brought to the workplace, none of which had anything to do with any of this. These women stepped forward to help and got slapped in the face. It was very easy for them to contact the two journalists that had covered the story and ensure the letter and its performative response made it into their hands.

The onslaught continued.

Chapter 47

"You have to have confidence in your ability, and then be tough enough to follow through." Rosalynn Carter

January 2021 started the new year off HOT.

The media coverage of United Way was relentless. On January 11, the *HuffPost* covered not only the letter written by the former employees but also an incident from another former employee, who had posted on LinkedIn and Twitter that she experienced misogyny, sexism, and "even so far as to assault" while working at United Way. She told *HuffPost* that she had gone to HR twice at United Way Worldwide to report what had happened to her, only to be told to rethink whether she wanted to come forward. I was familiar with her story, and it is horrific. I was actually able to speak to this woman. She was, in fact, assaulted: physically twice, by high-ranking males at United Way Worldwide. One of them is now the CEO of a local United Way.

United Way Worldwide told *HuffPost* they were investigating the matter following the claims that were made in the November 23 article but declined to provide any further details.[6] The board continued their pathetic line: "As shared before, United Way Worldwide (UWW)

---

[6] https://www.huffpost.com/entry/united-way-former-employees-letter-harassment-discrimination_n_5ff5c73cc5b6ea7351c6fc72

is deeply disturbed by any allegations of misconduct and is conducting a comprehensive investigation into our culture and the process by which the recent allegations of misconduct were handled," stating that they were "committed to completing the investigation as expeditiously as possible."

Julie, nor any of the five former employees she was in contact with about the letter to the board, ever heard from investigators. Nor did Ana, me, or the third woman on the initial *HuffPost* article.

My statement to the Huff Post was that "I haven't been contacted and don't anticipate I will be; they don't want to hear the truth." To paraphrase Jack Nicholson's infamous line from the movie *A Few Good Men*, "They didn't want the truth because they couldn't handle the truth." The leadership was rotten at its core, like a bad apple, and if the board didn't acknowledge that, they wouldn't have to deal with it.

On January 29, *HuffPost's* headline proclaimed, "United Way CEO's Fate Uncertain Amid Growing Crisis at The Nonprofit... organization is facing financial trouble as investigators look into a culture of sexual harassment and retaliation that he allegedly fostered."[7] Emily's article detailed how as many as 220 local chapters of the United Way had stopped paying dues to the organization's home office, United Way Worldwide, cutting off a crucial source of funding during a time of layoffs and uncertainty for the major non-profit. She spoke to both current and former employees and local market CEOs who were familiar with discussions indicating the CEO's fate was uncertain. According to a current employee at a major branch of the

---

[7] https://www.huffpost.com/entry/united-way-worldwide-ceo-brian-gallagher-crisis_n_60130fe2c5b622df90f19e75

non-profit, the United Way Worldwide board was scheduled to meet the following Thursday, February 6, to discuss whether it was time for him to exit.

I was so happy to read in the comments "That he hasn't already been dismissed says a lot," the employee said, pointing to complaints about the culture inside the organization, and that, "He should've gone a long time ago," a former employee told *HuffPost*. "Patriarchy doing what patriarchy gonna do: Dig their heels in."

United Way also told Emily when she contacted them for a statement that it had hired a law firm to investigate the culture and claims but had not yet released any findings, and that the investigation into the harassment allegations is "scheduled to conclude shortly."

Still, none of us had been contacted, and it didn't look like we would be. When conducting a proper investigation, a neutral third party speaks to all other parties involved. In this case, the law firm who was retained, notorious for "whitewashing" harassment claims in the private sector, was operating at the behest of the board, who had a vested interest in the outcome. The board members clearly did not understand that their obligation was to the organization itself, not the CEO. I sit on boards; I've been in the same position. The board chair is the "boss" of the CEO in an organization. If any other employee besides the CEO had behaved this way and retaliated against someone for reporting something, that employee would be investigated and likely gone. This CEO exhibited all the behavioral traits of a classic narcissist and was arrogant enough to think the rules didn't apply to him—and the board seemed to go along with this.

Others shared with me that during a United Way town hall meeting with all the staff, someone inquired of the

CEO if he was willing to take a leave of absence while the investigation played out so as not to cause a PR issue and further distraction. His response? "If you think I'm going to sit on the sidelines and not get paid during all this, guess again. NO!" This was also the same person who on multiple occasions would stand up in front of staff and say things like, "Since my oldest daughter is dating an African American and I might have black grandkids, we should probably look at Diversity as a key initiative."

Performative wokeness as its best.

The *HuffPost* further reported that United Way Worldwide had laid off staff and announced pay cuts for higher-level positions the week before the article was published. United Way told *HuffPost* that salary reductions were "temporary" for senior staff. I know from insiders that the cuts were twenty-five percent—that's a lot. Another source familiar with the situation cited that there would be more layoffs next month and that employees were also told they might be able to voluntarily resign and receive severance.

Per usual, United Way tried to deflect with the following statement, "United Way Worldwide has not been immune to the impacts of the COVID-19 pandemic and the resulting economic fallout; and the protracted nature of this downturn has forced us to make difficult decisions."

United Way Worldwide was able to get a $4.8 million Payroll Protection Program loan[8] from the Federal government in April 2020, part of the federal government's

---

[8] https://www.sba.com/ppp-funded-companies/virginia/united-way-worldwide-7016010#:~:text=UNITED%20WAY%20WORLDWIDE%20%20%20Loan%20Amount%20,%20Non-Profit%20Organization%20%2010%20more%20rows%20

Chapter 47

COVID-19 relief package, which offered the loans as a means to mitigate firms avoid laying-off employees.

The deception became clear when Emily received an internal email that had been sent to the communications staff at a local United Way alleging the pandemic wasn't the issue for United Way; the source called the COVID-19 talking point "untrue."

Making matters worse, the local United Ways were furious because the Salesforce platform that the CEO had touted as the silver bullet was a mess (by the way, that was *Harasshole's* project). He was seeking to subsidize the investment by raising dues from the local United Ways. Remember, that was the December 2019 project that made me forego my time off, yet the COO was nowhere to be found like the rest of the executive team was "Dialing for Dollars," contacting the locals to sell them on why this was great.

The publicity of my situation and the public airing of the dirty laundry about the toxic culture only stoked the local United Way CEOs more. Withholding dues from Worldwide was the only measure the local United Ways had to fight back; and dues composed the vast majority of Worldwide's revenue stream.

In short, the network was calling for accountability from Worldwide on financial, reputational, and cultural issues. They were acknowledging poor leadership at the top and quietly, but surely, calling for change.

Chapter 48

"You can fall, but you can rise also."
Angelique Kidjo

It had been a month since I had submitted my paperwork to the EEOC; I hadn't heard anything back yet.

I thought the shit had kind of hit the fan by this point with the media coverage. Apparently, it had not; not yet, at least.

In my household, the nearly weekly Friday coverage of United Way came to be known as the "Friday kick-in-the-Balls" to United Way from *HuffPost*. From a publicity perspective, Fridays are the days when you want negative stories to appear (well, you really NEVER want a negative story to occur, but if it does, Friday is the optimal time) as they'll fade away over the weekend. In this case, the opposite proved true, and online forum discussions lasted for days after the story went live. The comments posted were nothing if not consistent in negative perceptions of United Way. There was always the occasional troll who surfaced as one expects in every form of social media today. One comment that has stuck with me simply because of how far out there it was stated that "the author (Emily Peck) should have disclosed her relationship (personal) with one of the accusers." Presumably, the reader was referring to Ana, me, or the third anonymous woman. I can assure you, none of us had a personal relationship or any other relationship with Emily. To this day, none of us have ever met her or even had so much as a visual interaction with her. Aside from her picture on her social profiles, I wouldn't recognize her if she were standing next to me on the street. Although these days, with masks on, I also don't recognize many other people, either.

Chapter 49

"You may encounter many defeats, but you must not be defeated. In fact, it may be necessary to encounter the defeats, so you can know who you are, what you can rise from, how you can still come out of it."
Maya Angelou

And true to form, the following Friday didn't disappoint. On February 5, 2021, I woke up to a *HuffPost* headline that read:

"United Way Worldwide Releases Sham Internal Investigation

One of the largest non-profits in the country says it's in the clear when it comes to sexual harassment allegations. Its own documents show otherwise."

Business Insider followed suit with:

> "United Way concluded it didn't retaliate against women who alleged harassment, but three women who filed complaints said no one contacted them for the investigation."

Both articles detailed a poorly conducted investigation in which the outcome was pre-determined and intended to clear the organization of any wrongdoing in both the court of public opinion and its own network.

United Way's public stance was that the investigation carried out by a third-party law firm at the behest of United Way Worldwide found "the employment decisions made with respect to the three employees at issue were found to be based on legitimate, non-discriminatory, and non-retaliatory reasons." Other than retaliation, there WAS no cause to terminate me. It seemed to me that the fact that they had settled with Ana was an admission of guilt. You don't settle and have someone sign an NDA when there is nothing to hide. My EEOC charges and that of the third woman were also still pending.

United Way publicly disclosed that the investigating law firm reached out twice to all current employees, and only twenty had responded, less than ten percent of the total employee headcount. Honestly, when people are working within a retaliatory culture, do you think they're going to speak up?

Both national publications slammed United Way Worldwide. Outside experts with whom both publications consulted for their reporting had also concurred that the investigation was not done properly. *HuffPost* had even obtained documents that showed the law firm did not review the actual substance and material facts of our complaints at all; the law firm was only hired to examine how the organization handled the complaints. Furthermore, UWW also released a bunch of internal documents that were sent to me by people on the "inside" and contained many inaccuracies, if not outright and deliberate mistruths. *HuffPost* secured an employment lawyer who works on discrimination and harassment cases to review reviewed United Way's press release in which it had claimed it was cleared of charges. The attorney's stated public opinion was simply, "It's self-serving propaganda."

In an internal Q & A document released by United Way, in response to a question regarding why the former employees who made the complaints weren't addressed, the response was that the primary mandate of the investigation was to assess HOW the organization investigated the complaints, not the complaints themselves, even though they had enough information to conclude that the complaints were indeed "valid." The information consisted of speaking to about 20 employees and reviewing 2,500 pages of documents, primarily policies, and procedures as well as a few complaints that had been submitted to the Ethics Hotline, personnel records, and employee surveys.

The Ethics Hotline was a "confidential" third party that one could contact to anonymously lodge a complaint or raise a concern about suspected unethical or illegal behavior. What is so telling in this is that the complaints of the three of us who filed with the EEOC were not made through the Ethics Hotline, the policies and procedures were clearly NOT followed, or *Harasshole* would have been long gone, employee surveys have nothing to do with this (I know—I oversaw the group that conducted them and am very familiar with the content of them) and as for personnel records, well, if there was anything negative in mine (which to the very best of my knowledge there wasn't) I was NEVER made aware of it or spoken to about it. According to their own accounts, neither were Ana nor the third woman. As the third woman reported directly to me, had there been a severe or serious complaint that was in her personnel file, I would have, or certainly should have, been made aware.

In the world of marketing and communications, this is what's known as "spin." And spinning they were—they still couldn't get their story straight and hadn't been able to from the start because it was just that, a story, by definition, "an account of an imaginary or real event or people...."

They were getting crucified by the local United Ways as well, who weren't buying the line of crap Worldwide was peddling. United Way Worldwide exists primarily to serve its own network. It does minimal fundraising on its own; there are few national programs and does not provide a direct service in any way. Rather it provides operational and back-office support for the local chapters, who are really the first line customer. And they were not happy.

"A loss of confidence in CEO's leadership had already been a feeling shared by many [local United Ways]," read a letter sent to the Worldwide office on behalf of the leaders of thirty-three local United Ways. "To accept the conclusion that United Way Worldwide bears no fault or responsibility, you would have to believe that several former employees got together, created an untrue story and gave up their jobs (in some cases) or risked them (in other cases) and decided to drag United Way Worldwide through the public mud. That seems like a lot of effort if you are happy and feel valued in your job," the letter added.

Chapter 50

"If you think you can't change the world, it just means you're not one of those that will."
Jacques Fresco

Happy birthday, to me...
February 9, 2021.

Another trip around the sun. Older and, for sure, wiser. The sun rose like it did on any and every other day. I started it in the same way that I started every morning: a workout and COFFEE. I love my coffee. We've already talked about that. There's something special about the smell of it brewing and the taste of the first sip as it injects caffeine into my system.

The birthday calls, texts, and emails streamed in steadily. Among the calls that I had that day, one was an interview with a researcher doing a study on the true cost of sexual harassment.

That afternoon, I decided to take Mojo for a walk. It was full-on sunny and not too cold. I recalled my state of mind on my last birthday and the events that had just transpired, I and thought to myself about how quickly the year had flown by.

Mojo was saddled up and pacing in circles by the front door, ready to go. I locked the door, and we set off. Never do I leave my house, even to walk him, without a phone in hand. That day though, I forgot my phone.

When I came back into my home office after we finished our walk, my phone was ringing. After that call, it didn't stop for almost seven hours.

"Lisa," Emily's voice spoke with some urgency on the other end of the phone, "I need a quote from you, like now."

Huh? What? My brain wasn't processing. At all. "Why? What's going on, Emily?" I asked in confusion.

"The news just broke," she replied, "the CEO is out. Wanna give me a statement?"

My heartbeat increased, and I smiled so big I think Emily could hear it stretching across my face all the way from New York. "I'm thankful for the change in leadership, so United Way can continue the good work that they do," was all I could think to say at the time. Emily hung up—she needed to publish the article.

I let out a scream. A loud, long scream. I don't know if it was a scream of relief, joy, or just shock. I never had a moment to process it because my phone started immediately blowing up. Calls, texts, emails were piling in faster than I could read or respond. Other reporters were calling for statements; *Business Insider* and the trade publications that cover the philanthropic sector, including the *Chronicle of Philanthropy* and *The Nonprofit Times*. Not surprisingly, this was huge news to them.

H-O-L-Y SHIT.

Had this seriously just happened, and what was the back story?

To this day, I don't know what really happened. It was positioned as a "resignation," one that was "planned, in anticipation of retirement," but was then escalated to an earlier date. I know the CEO. I know his ego. I do not believe he willingly resigned. I very much suspect the board finally

Chapter 50

realized that the organization couldn't withstand any more pressure from the media or the network without acting to mitigate the risk of corporate partners starting to pull away so as not to get United Way's stink on them.

I'll never know the truth, and if this says anything about me and who I am as a person, honestly, I was conflicted emotionally. There was the part of me that was happy, like the best birthday gift EVER had just been handed to me, and justice had sort of been done. An eye for an eye, right? The other part of me felt, and I can't believe it, bad for the CEO. His role at United Way—his job—was his life; this was all he had ever known. His vision was to go out in glory at the time of his choosing with a big party, with all the head honchos from global organizations there to celebrate him. Instead, he slunk out with his tail between his legs, publicly disgraced. Knowing this man as I do, I can assure you he is playing the victim, even today, and that there is black hatred for me deep in his soul.

Over the next few weeks, I received congratulatory messages from people for "taking him down." I didn't take him down—he made his own bed. Someone reminded me very kindly the other day, "Lisa, you didn't create a problem for United Way. United Way created their own problem."

What I *was* proud of and saw as a victory was my own strength in doing this and raising visibility in an attempt to prevent it from happening to someone else. This wasn't the end, though. There had still been no accountability, no settlement. And I was determined I'd see this through to the very end, even if it meant having to sue United Way.

The CEO's last day was scheduled for March 1, 2021. A few weeks prior, people inside United Way started leaving and getting laid off; the organization lost some very good people during this period. Part of the headcount reduction was to first offer voluntary buyouts to people in the organization who were deemed "eligible." Two of those people were the COO and *Harasshole*. They got buyout packages to move on—ZERO ACCOUNTABILITY. Rewarded for bad behavior. The COO wrote an insincere note to the staff about how much she valued the work United Way did, even though saving her own back was clearly a priority since she quickly popped up as the SVP of HR at a major restaurant chain just two weeks after leaving United Way. You don't get that kind of job during a pandemic overnight, so she had obviously been planning to leave. The press release talked glowingly about the great culture she had built across the United Way network. Her role was only Worldwide, and she clearly did not build a great culture at UWW. I hope they know what they got. Suffice it to say; I'll never eat another Bloomin' Onion again—you can figure it out.

My sources tell me the CEO snuck out without saying a single word. After forty years in the network, the CEO didn't even pen a letter to the network or staff thanking those who had helped or supported him along the way.

As for *Harasshole*, he also left silently. I don't know where he is now, but I worry that wherever he's at, he'll do this again, and someone else will fall prey to a problem that will likely go unaddressed; sadly, that seems to be the way of the world today.

We can ask all kinds of things on a candidate form when applying for a job, we can run background checks and check references, but there's no safety net to catch this kind of bad behavior in HR systems or processes; that in itself is a problem, but even worse, it allows behavior like this to run unchecked. It's why *Harasshole* is a serial harasser, because he gets away with it, and nobody stops him.

Chapter 51

"Do not tame the wolf inside you just because you've met someone who doesn't have the courage to handle you."
Belle Estreller

While consumed by the legal aspects of the case and publicity swarming around it, the reality was that I still needed a job. And I needed one fast. In early January, after months of searching for a job in the middle of a global pandemic, I was contacted by a recruiter for a role that appeared perfect for me. When I was terminated, I had assumed that it would take me a solid six months to find a job under normal circumstances. Now we were living in anything but that. While I hadn't been looking to stay in the non-profit sector (at all), this was a global role with a team larger than my former one and direct responsibility for revenue generation, too. It would provide me with a great opportunity to stretch my career into new areas. As the media had just "gone live," so to speak, my story was front and center. I thus decided to share with the recruiter, who worked for one of the "Big 5" as they're known, in confidence, the terms of my departure from United Way. She was not only empathetic but assured me that the CEO of the organization would be as well; in fact, she, the CEO, had dealt with this as well. I exhaled.

I was progressing in the interview process for the Chief Marketing and Development Officer role at the non-profit organization. By this point, I had met with the CEO a couple of times. We talked briefly about my departure from United Way, and she shared that she, too, had been a #MeToo and respected my courage to stand up and speak out. The more I learned about the organization and its mission, the more excited I became. This represented an excellent growth opportunity that would allow me to continue to develop professionally by expanding my role into areas I had previously not been involved in, as well as overseeing a team that would be larger than the one I had previously managed. Even better, this non-profit dealt with animals, not people, so that was a huge plus, given my current emotional state.

By late March, I'd been through all the interviews with the entire executive team, members of the team I would lead, and all of my references had been checked. It was clear I was the lead candidate. I was excited at the prospect of getting back to work. While I was keeping busy with advisory board work and some light consulting, it wasn't the same as having a "real" job.

The culture of the company was a critical factor for me as I made my decision about where to go next, especially given what I'd just gone through. While researching the organization, I was aware they #TheyToo had had a #MeToo issue several years prior. Unlike United Way, they addressed it immediately and appropriately. The current CEO had been one of the survivors of that situation, and I respected her for successfully navigating it and landing where she did. But, the fact that she let this situation happen to me resulted in my losing any respect for her that I had had.

Note that I do not use the word victim here—I almost never use this term—to describe those who have endured sexual harassment or retaliation in the workplace. My mindset is that you can either be a victim or a survivor; I choose the latter. **I will not be a victim.**

I've never actually had a female boss, ever. However, what I had discovered over the course of the interview process, and conversations with the CEO, was that she was calm, seemingly compassionate, and appeared to have the respect of her staff—all important characteristics.

The CEO made me a verbal offer during a conversation we had in late March or early April, and after a short round of negotiation, I was satisfied. It was not only a good offer but represented a good opportunity with room for me to develop professionally.

Before the written offer was extended, she asked that I speak with a few of their board members to avoid the perception that she had made a hire without them having a chance to speak with me. For a role like this, I had expected—even assumed—that I would meet with the board prior to an offer, whether it be verbal or written. Nevertheless, the CEO was emphatic that these calls were only out of courtesy, and not interviews. The decision was hers to make, and she had made it.

The calls were scheduled for the first week of April, with two on a Monday evening via Zoom. The following morning, I spoke to the CEO and was assured the calls went fine, though she still offered a bit of non-material guidance for the subsequent two calls. While nothing more than the names of the people to whom I'd be speaking with was provided, I had researched them and felt like I was ready.

However, I was so NOT ready for what happened on the third call, which took place on a Thursday evening with the board member who headed up the CMO practice at the recruiting firm. I knew something was "off" from the minute the Zoom window opened. She was rude, unprepared, and, frankly, openly hostile. She did not have my resume in front of her and clearly hadn't so much as even glanced at it. She printed it while we were on the call, nearly knocking over her printer in the process.

As she flipped through the pages of my resume in her visible agitation, she asked, "Did you even go to college because I can't find anything about your education on your resume." As my head said, "This lady looks at resumes all day long for a living, and she can't find my education, AND she was just that rude to me?" my mouth responded calmly, "It's at the bottom of the second page."

She controlled the conversation, rapid-firing questions at me, barely giving me a chance to respond and quite frankly, showing me that she knew little about either the strategic plan or the current state of the organization based on her line of questioning.

As we neared the end of the allocated time, she asked if I had any questions for her. I did, but she had not left time. I asked just one: why she chose to allocate her time and talent to this organization vs. any other.

I had unknowingly just poured gasoline on a smoldering ember. I can't do justice to the response in written form; it truly needs a verbal tone inflected to understand it completely. Quite simply, I was told that she was brought in to oversee the governance process, a standard function on any properly established and run board, which was a result of an... ahem... "little issue" the organization had encountered. "But," she assumed, "I was very familiar with that as it appeared that I, too, had a similar 'issue'." And there it was, blatantly out in the open. It was now clear that she had a problem with the fact that I spoke out and thus perceived me to be a troublemaker.

Chapter 51

For those currently facing harassment or retaliation at work, hear this LOUD AND CLEAR: YOU ARE NOT THE PROBLEM. Unless you are the perpetrator, of course, don't you dare let anyone make you out to be the problem or believe you ARE the problem. This is a typical example of gaslighting, a tactic used to make you question your own reality.

Okay, so this call hadn't gone well, but the first two had, and there was still one more. I had been vetted, interviewed; reference checked seven ways to Sunday.

The following afternoon, at the end of the first week of April 2021, I had a call with the fourth and final board member. He was the antithesis of the woman I spoke to the day before. We had a great conversation that extended past the allocated time, talking about things such as branding challenges and cures.

Despite how positive this final call was, the situation with the one female board member was really bothering me. I reached out to the CEO Monday morning. When we finally connected, she withdrew the offer. The female board member had leveraged an argument against which the CEO wasn't necessarily able to offer a defense, which was that I didn't have the skills to do the job.

Here is what I will tell you about that—not true. This organization was considerably smaller than United Way and with a much, much tighter focus. Their business issues were the same ones I had confronted and successfully solved at United Way. Was the team a bit bigger? Yes. Could I handle that? Of course. I'd managed teams larger than the one I had at United Way in past roles. Was there a revenue piece for which I had not had any direct responsibility for oversight in one of my previous positions? Yes. Had I done a sufficient job of communicating via an interview process that spanned

FIVE MONTHS that I was qualified, especially since I had an offer? Clearly.

The board member knew she couldn't attack me on my "issue," as she put it, because of the CEO's prior experience. But clearly, she was gunning for me from minute one. She hadn't so much as reviewed my resume, so that was a tip-off. What the CEO told me that was that "the woman hadn't really liked me and didn't feel I could do the job, so proceeding forward would make the situation untenable for both of us."

At this point, with nothing to lose except the job that had just been taken away, I told the CEO exactly what had happened. I explained to her the interaction I had had with the board member, her tone, what she had specifically said to me, and the line of questioning that had so clearly indicated she did not understand the business, while I, as a lowly candidate, who had basically accused her of not having skills to do the job, clearly demonstrated that I understood and knew how to address it.

The response? A quiet and slow, "Oh, my God." No apology, no nothing. This was a CEO who clearly could not handle her board and was not able to stand her ground, either to them or for what was right. Disappointing.

Chapter 52

"Life is too short to wake up with regrets. So love the people who treat you right. Forgive the ones that don't and believe that everything happens for a reason."
Dr. Seuss

While I later realized that I had, in fact, dodged a bullet, at the time, it threw me into a bad state of three-week-long depression. I had withdrawn from other searches for roles I had been equally interested in as this one neared its final state, and I determined it to be my role of choice. What upset me further was that the rejection came from yet another woman who didn't see any obligation to help when everybody, including her firm, was busy talking about the value of women.

I had already experienced a female COO not defending me against harassment. Further, a female board chair neither addressing or acknowledging the issue. And here, a female board member had a problem with the fact that I spoke up, and a female CEO, who had herself been in a similar circumstance, caved to pressure she knew was bullshit. So much for women supporting each other.

Women United, United Way's Affinity Group of female donors and volunteers, stood silently—all 70,000 of them. Not a single one expressed concern or outrage that the organization for which they had collectively and cumulatively raised $2 billion had not one but THREE

EEOC charges filed by female employees in a single year. They stood by silently while they professed their support for the organization's initiatives that were oriented toward women. Hypocrites. All of them. Sisters, DO BETTER. There's a saying about if you see another woman's crown tilted, straighten it for her. In today's environment, too many women are busy knocking crowns off each other's heads.

Speaking of women not supporting women, United Way's U.S. President of Operations was another one. I shared with you earlier how, during the retreat the week after I got fired, she accosted me in the ladies' room. At the end of March 2021, I received a text out of the blue from her, asking if I was "up for a conversation?" I was really curious and, in my naïveté, thought perhaps she'd been dispatched by the Board for cleanup on aisle five now that the three amigos were gone. Why, why, why do I always assume people operate with good intentions and do the right thing? I should have learned by now. Trust, my fatal flaw.

After consulting my attorney, I agreed to converse with her. It was terribly awkward. My role was to simply listen—I truly had nothing to say, and she had been the one to initiate the outreach. In short, she apologized (a year later!) for not being aware of what was happening and not supporting me. Even though she did say, "I'm sorry," I did not acknowledge nor accept her weak attempt at an apology—if that's even what it was.

I had to call her on the carpet, reminding her that she actually WAS aware. She had witnessed the CEO's behavior towards me. She had outwardly admitted she knew about my termination during our conversation in the restroom and that it was wrong. She was a bystander. She sat around and watched, never daring to put herself at risk by standing up for me. Self-preservation will always rule. She stumbled through the rest of the call; there wasn't much left to say. This might have been an attempt for her to clear her conscience or soul in some way. It had nothing to do with me. As a side note, during our call, she was effusive about the interim CEO, the board chair of the U.S. Board, and technically, her boss. Things were great; he was so much better than the former CEO etc., etc. Since that call, just six months after the departure of the CEO, COO, and *Harasshole,* she too left the organization. It says a lot for the belief that the culture was fine and nothing had happened.

Chapter 53

"One day in retrospect the years of struggle will strike you as the most beautiful."
Sigmund Freud

On May 11, my attorney and I had a video call with the EEOC investigator to answer a few questions. I had asked in advance if there was anything I could do to prepare and was told this was just a call to discuss the basics. I was professionally dressed, at least up top as the new norm for biz-via-video; I rocked a "business mullet"—profesh up top, workout shorts on the bottom.

As the investigator began asking questions to confirm his understanding of the documents, I felt my chest getting tight and tears starting to well up in my eyes. It had been over a year—why was I still feeling this way? I got so upset and was crying so hard that I had to turn off my camera.

I think what really hit me was both the unfairness of it all and the mourning of a role that I thought would be the last one in my career. I remember telling the CEO when I accepted the job on August 28, 2015, that I had spent the first fifteen years of my career at one company, UPS, and I intended to finish my career here, at United Way. I felt as if they stole my plans for the rest of my career.

There is a song by The Sundays (remember, I'm a child of the glorious musical decade that was the eighties, even though this was released in 1990) that has two lines I love.

The title line itself, which is also the chorus, "Here's where the story ends..." and "It's that little souvenir of a terrible year...."

I suppose that's perhaps what this book is!

Chapter 54

"What is coming is better than what is gone."
Arabic Proverb

I believe things happen for a reason, even if the reason isn't quite clear at a given moment time. I've told myself the reason is that the right thing (my next role) just hasn't come along yet. I needed to finish this book first, and I also realized that I was meant for something bigger and that the universe had a plan for me. Patience may be a virtue, but it definitely isn't one of mine. I have value to offer and I. AM. READY.

The irony is not lost on me that as I am finishing this manuscript during the 2021 Jewish High Holy Days. Beginning with Rosh Hashana, the start of the Jewish High Holy Days, which is our new year, and ending with Yom Kippur, the day of atonement, these are days for reflection. According to both Torah and tradition, we ask each other for forgiveness and give others forgiveness for their transgressions. Technically, if someone asks for our forgiveness, we're supposed to grant it, even if, deep down, we don't want to.

I woke up this morning thinking if I would honestly and sincerely be capable of granting forgiveness to those in the book (the CEO, *Harasshole*, or the COO) for their transgressions against me or if their actions are simply unforgivable?

For nearly two years, I've been emotionally, financially, and reputationally compromised in more ways than I can count. My health has suffered. My family has been impacted. All because these three people could not behave appropriately in the workplace and do the right thing. I don't have an answer to that question, and nor do I need to, because it's not going to be a scenario that plays out in reality.

Although my life has been shattered in a pandemic-ridden world, I've had time to reflect on what is really important to me in life. I have so much to be grateful for. I haven't lost anyone to COVID and have a roof over my head and food on the table. The virtual world has introduced me to many amazing people with whom my path may have never crossed.

I can't help but often think as I reflect on this journey that I believe things happen for a reason; this is not an experience I would have chosen (nor wished upon anyone else), but perhaps it chose me.

My story has become my purpose. To empower and teach others how to navigate; if the indicator on the map that shows YOU ARE HERE. We ALL have the power to effect positive change: each and every one of us. But often, we don't leverage that. As individuals who form a collective, when we add our voice to the chorus, we can get louder.

This is not the end of the story. There's a long road ahead, beginning with the EEOC making its determination and awarding me a Right to Sue with Cause letter. We'll see what happens. I cannot predict the future; I just hope that the universe will right itself. It has been two years since this story unfolded, and try as I might, despite the job market being on fire (according to the media), I have yet to secure a new role. Have I been blacklisted for standing up?

Stay strong,
Lisa

Chapter 55

"The more that you read, the more things you will know. The more that you learn, the more places you'll go."
Dr. Seuss

Here's my disclaimer on the following content. I'm not an attorney; I don't play one on TV, and I didn't stay at a Holiday Inn Express last night. These are things I've learned either through my own experience or via researching them. Use this simply as guidance or some things to think about, but always consult an attorney if you are unsure or uncomfortable with something. And do it early on—don't wait. It may be nothing, but when something doesn't feel right, it usually isn't.

FOR EMPLOYEES:
 Before taking a job or working for a company, do your research.
 Google is your friend. EEOC filings are not publicly available, but you can check to see if there's been any negative publicity or reports of allegations of bad behavior associated with the organization where you are seeking employment. It was during my research for the non-profit that yanked the job from me when I found out about their #MeToo issue and how it had been resolved.
 Ask to speak to current employees when considering a company as an employer of choice. Remember, you are

interviewing them as much as they are interviewing you. We've been wired to think it's a one-way process; it's not. Put it in the same perspective as them checking your references. Two caveats, though; make sure it's at the appropriate time in the process (I'd put in the request when they put in theirs for references), and remember, you aren't going to give them a reference who says anything bad about you, so they'll likely connect you with their shining stars.

Some questions you may want to consider are:

Regarding culture, do they exemplify what they talk about publicly? How? Can the employee give you an example?

Does the company live its values?

Has the employee ever had to go to HR on anything? Was it resolved to their satisfaction?

LinkedIn is also a great tool to leverage. Consider posting that you are looking at 'Company X' as an employer of choice and would like to speak with employees in confidence to learn more about the company. Make sure to #(hashtag) the company in your post so anyone following them will see it. Ask that current or former employees willing to talk with you send a private message, and you can use that forum to ask questions. You'll likely get a mix of people who are true brand ambassadors and want to promote the company and some who are disgruntled and may want to share why. I caution you to take it all with a grain of salt and simply use it as one data point in your overall diligence.

During the very final stages of the interview process, ask what documents you will be required to complete if you accept a role. Confidentiality and non-compete agreements are fairly standard. Companies will not provide these

Chapter 55

documents as part of the onboarding process for review until you are fully hired.

Congratulations on your new role!

Once you accept the role, take your time to review all the documents you are asked to sign very carefully. Wording that you want to be specifically on the lookout for is anything related to "Forced Arbitration" or "Mandatory Arbitration."

Arbitration is an alternative process of settling disputes within the legal system instead of using traditional litigation. Most people think of taking legal issues through the court system and the typical lengthy process where a judge and/or jury are used to decide the outcome of a case. Arbitration, however, is a different process where, similar to litigation, a third party (not a judge or jury) determines the outcome of a dispute. It occurs outside of a traditional courtroom setting, often in a conference room, or these days, over video.

But be careful. The company will tell you this is a quicker and less costly option. The things they don't tell you: In arbitration, the decision-maker, called an arbitrator, isn't always neutral and in many cases the company selects the arbitrator for you. The arbitor conducts a hearing, receives and reviews testimony and evidence from the parties involved (there are more limitations with regards to both the witnesses and testimony which are allowed in arbitration), and then decides the case. With arbitration, the number of cases found in favor of the employee are small, and there is no appeals process. Gretchen Carlson recently was successful in passing federal legislation that will allow employees a choice about this process instead of being forced into arbitration. Titled The Ending Forced Arbitration of Sexual Harassment Act of 2021, bills S.2342 and H.R. 4445 aim to change how behavior is hidden by making the process illegal in cases of sexual harassment and/or assault. Although they often come from the legal field, arbitrators are not required to be licensed attorneys.

In a situation where there is a dispute, you may have the option of deciding whether to use arbitration instead of going to court—unless your paperwork states forced arbitration which makes it mandatory to solve conflicts via this process. This is known as a "forced arbitration clause."

If you have an employment contract, which many more senior people do, look at the termination language; what does it specify for severance if you are terminated? Often, there is language that gives a company an "out" if you are terminated for cause; however, cause language can be very ambiguous.

Most companies will not allow you to negotiate on these terms; remember, the reason they have you sign these papers is to protect the company. And a word of caution, sorry to all my Human Resources peeps out there, but please don't make the mistake I did; HR is not your friend. While they often have really great names for this department, like "People & Culture," "Talent Management," or "Employee Services," this is branding. Plain and simple. Human Resources is there to PROTECT THE COMPANY. I don't say this to demean or disparage those who work in HR or the function itself; it's a simple fact that most people lose sight of. Like Marketing, like Finance, they are there for the company, not YOU, regardless of what they are called.

It's okay to sign these papers in most cases—you have no choice if you want the job, but know and understand what you signed.

Chapter 55

Houston, we have a problem....

If you start to have a problem with someone, don't dismiss it; you never know if an isolated comment is the start of a pattern of behavior, and you want to ensure you keep a good paper trail—documentation is critical. And don't do it via your company email!

Use your phone to send yourself an email detailing the incident that occurred, the time and location, and who may have witnessed it. Be as specific as possible. I have a good memory, but I still documented everything. You may want to consider including other details, too, like how the interaction or event made you feel. I would just email myself and keep them all in a folder; it was very helpful when I needed to go back and construct a timeline of incidents. It was actually in the process of reviewing all those emails that I realized that what had happened was retaliation.

Should things get so serious that you encounter health issues or a diagnosis from your doctor that you believe are directly related to whatever you are experiencing, keep solid records of everything, including any time missed from work for doctor's appointments.

When possible, try and have a witness. You don't want to make a big deal out of it or drag people into your business, but if there is possibly someone you trust, it would be a good option to have them present. When *Harasshole* accosted me outside of my office, I asked the HR Director, whose office was three down from mine, if she had heard it and then shared what had just happened with her. You will recall that I also sent an email documenting the event at the conference to the woman with whom I was speaking when *Harasshole* commented on how my skirt fit me in front of her.

Be very clear in confronting your *Harasshole* and letting them know that their behavior is not okay. This is a hard thing to do and can be scary. You may be gaslighted into thinking you heard something wrong or misinterpreted it. If it happens once—okay, maybe so. Repeatedly—no, you didn't imagine it.

With mine, initially, I didn't respond, assuming my silence or refusal to respond would shut it down. It didn't. The next tactic was that whenever he made a comment, I'd very pointedly tell him, "*Harasshole*, we are not here to talk about my outfit of the day (or insert any number of things). The stated objective for our interaction is to accomplish X." If nothing else, it lets them know that you heard what they said, stated that it's not okay and that this is a business engagement. If you think you can do it, tell the perpetrator very directly, "What you just said/did is NOT OK. It's harassment. We have a policy that governs that, and you are violating it—please stop and don't do it again."

I get that this can be hard. It's confrontational, and in the event that this person is a superior to you, it's tough. That's why the women on my team shared what had happened with their direct manager and me. There was zero chance that either of them, as more junior and women of color, would go up against a white male member of the C-Suite. Sad, but true.

As the first line of defense before you go to HR, or if you aren't comfortable going there, you have a few options. Almost all companies have an Ethics Hotline; the contact information for this line has to be posted somewhere by law. It's usually near a break area or perhaps an elevator. These lines are confidential, or at least they are supposed to be, and should allow you to be anonymous. Depending on the structure of your HR Policies, you may also choose to share this with someone else, who, by policy, may be obligated to report it. At United Way, and I'm paraphrasing, our policy stated that if it was even a suspected case of harassment, it had to be reported, and failure to do so could result in termination.

At some point, you will need to engage Human Resources. My advice, do it in writing first, so it's documented.

> "Dear HR,
> I am requesting a confidential meeting with you to specifically discuss an incident involving (NAME) that occurred on (DATE). This incident involved (specifics of what happened) which I believe is a violation of our policy governing _____."

Once you've met with HR, follow up with an email documenting your understanding of the conversation and any actions, steps, or guidance that are to be taken either by you or them.

Request that HR put this email and the one initiating the meeting you requested in your HR file and have them confirm they've done so.

Learn from my mistake on this one—don't wait until the company decides to act against you before securing an attorney. If things are turning south and it's not looking good, get counsel. For example, had I engaged counsel during this process, I likely would have been advised to file with the EEOC while still employed; you may be able to proactively negotiate an exit on your terms if that's what you are seeking.

"You're Fired!"

Hit the road, Jack (or Jill), and don't you come back. It's important to remember and acknowledge that Jacks also can get harassed or retaliated against. At one point, when

I was anonymously sharing others' stories of harassment on LinkedIn to use my voice for them, I had a guy share a story of his female boss getting him drunk at an event and assaulting him in a car. It happens.

If you are terminated, first things first: DO NOT SIGN ANYTHING. You will receive separation paperwork. If you are forty or older (there aren't many benefits to that, but this is one of them), by law, you must be given at least twenty-one days to sign a severance agreement and seven days to reconsider or revoke the signature.

Make sure any and all discussions you have with HR moving forward are in writing. I had a phone call with the COO as we were discussing the specifics of my departure the week following the receipt of my severance notice. She verbally assured me I would receive my bonus. I asked her for that in writing. When I did not receive it, I sent her a note seeking confirmation of our conversation. No response. Needless to say, I've incurred legal fees to try and recoup the over $36,000 I rightfully earned.

Either you or your attorney on your behalf, should request a copy of your personnel file. You have a right to know what's in there.

Silence is golden, or so the saying goes. Your severance offer will come with a Non-Disclosure Agreement (NDA) that governs your silence about the company, this situation, and likely other topics as well. You almost assuredly signed a confidentiality agreement upon hire. Now that you're terminated, that doesn't apply; you're no longer an employee. There are two reasons companies insist on NDAs: to protect business intelligence like trade secrets, intellectual property, and the like; the second is to hide bad behavior. They will hold your severance pay hostage for the signing of an NDA and agreeing not to pursue anything in court. You'll waive your rights to do so in the agreement you sign. My guidance is to negotiate the NDA. Here's why: agreeing not to disclose business information is the right thing to do. Even if you've been wronged—and this is tough, I know—do the right thing. It's not an argument you are going to win. However, you should own your experience. There are ways to navigate that, and there are a variety of approaches that you can take. For example, Ana's NDA allowed her to speak broadly about systemic issues. You need to decide if this is a topic that you are comfortable being silent about, but know that's how these issues continue to happen—companies bury them.

Gretchen Carlson's organization, Lift Our Voices (www.liftourvoices.org), has a mission of banning NDAs and forced arbitration clauses.

If a company has no bad behavior to hide, why do they need to ban speaking about it? Just sayin'.

It's Not Me

Perhaps you aren't dealing with a *Harasshole* directly, but you know someone who is. Do you know how to help them? Bystander intervention training teaches this and is part of my recommendations for companies. We need to empower people to hold each other accountable. The HR folks will hate me for this, but truly, it will help reduce instances if done right.

There are multiple Bystander Intervention frameworks sometimes using the 3Ds: Direct, Distract, Delegate, or even the newer 5Ds, which include Delay and Document. A great resource for this is iHollaback.org which offers training to both individuals and companies.

Here's a quick primer for you.

Direct: Call it as you see it. Point out threatening or inappropriate behavior in a safe, respectful manner. "That comment was demeaning to women and not funny. We don't speak that way here."

Distract: Draw away or divert attention. Make up an excuse to help your co-worker get away from their *Harasshole*. "Hey Dawn, I'm glad I ran into you. I had e-mailed you earlier about Project X with a critical question. Can I borrow you for a minute to speak with me about it?"

Delegate: Appoint someone else to help intervene. Similar to distract, this is where you get someone else to help. Depending on the situation and who the *Harasshole* is, you may want to ask a trusted colleague or even your boss to intervene and tell the *Harasshole* to stop that behavior.

Delay: Not in the actual moment, but when you witnessed harassment or some other inappropriate behavior and were unable to intervene at the time it occurred; check-in on the person and make sure they are okay. Acknowledge what you saw and ask if there is anything you can do to help. This would have been invaluable to me if someone had known to do it or actually done it.

Document: Depending on the situation and local laws, you may be in a position to document the interaction you see by taking a video or audio recording of it. DO NOT EVER post it online. Simply offer it to the person who was being harassed if they'd like it. This is really the last option; it can lead to legal ramifications, as well as other consequences that may have a severe impact on the person being harassed if it gets out.

This isn't all about you, sorry. Your employers also have some obligations to do things better here. Training is great, but it's a check the box item to mitigate risk. Our training at United Way included all this policy stuff, but if nobody enforces or follows the policy, what's the point?

FOR EMPLOYERS:

I was obligated, by policy, to speak up. What was United Way's obligation to me? After all, isn't the workplace in and of itself a contractual arrangement? I do work, and you pay me a fair wage for it? What about if I report bad behavior, and you do what...? Make me the bad guy and allow my *Harasshole* to proceed with zero consequences?

I've worked in the Human Resources function, but never as a practitioner. I've been a customer of the "People" function. It's really hard, in my opinion, to overstate the benefits that come to workplaces where people are willing to speak up. Ranging from improved team performance to innovation, to employee satisfaction, when employees believe that it's not safe to speak up, their colleagues and companies are at greater risk of reputational and brand damage, engagement stagnation, and churn leading to loss of institutional knowledge. When people conclude that it's just not worth it to speak up truthfully about problems, offer ideas, or ask questions with the goal of improvement, that organization is in trouble.

As these issues continue to come to light in the media weekly, if not daily, the gap between the kind of leaders and organizations we ought to have and the ones we have is expanding, not contracting.

Instead of responding in ways that lead employees to believe that speaking up is pointless or will damage them, organizations must find ways to reward the call-out of bad behavior as it benefits the company. There is a middle-ground between the idea that "HR's job is to protect the company," and "HR is not your friend."

PR-Event™ is a multi-tactical approach I've aggregated in an effort to ensure that you don't have a PR event like my former employer, who handled this poorly at every step possible. Here are the steps I believe organizations can take to make it easier for employees to speak up and report bad behavior without fear of retaliation.

1. TRAIN AND DEVELOP YOUR LEADERS ON CREATING AN ENVIRONMENT OF PSYCHOLOGICAL SAFETY

Most people are thrown into corporate management and leadership roles because they were good in their previous roles. But there is generally little overlap between the skills needed to be a good employee and those required to manage a team.

Think about this—Friday, someone is "Joe Employee" and gets promoted at the end of the day. They spend the weekend celebrating with family and/or friends and updating their LinkedIn profiles. Monday, they return to work as a team lead. They're now managing others. I promise you, as I've seen this happen along my career way too many times, nothing changed over the weekend other than their title.

If organizations invested more in developing critical leadership skills, including teaching leaders how to create an inclusive climate (and not one that's DEI oriented inclusivity, there is a difference here), where people feel free to speak up and report sensitive issues, they would improve not just that individual but also the team's effectiveness, and the overall organizational culture.

When people and the teams on which they work lack trust, they lack safety. Fear of safety impacts creativity, productivity, and willingness to experiment, which is a necessary part of innovation. And after these last eighteen months, we've all seen that innovation, creativity, and agility are key to business survival.

2. SELECT LEADERS WHO HAVE INTEGRITY AND COMPETENCE; SOFT SKILLS COUNT, TOO

Although leadership development is critical, the best predictor of how well managers and leaders respond to any training or intervention tactics is how much potential they have in the first place.

If organizations spent more time carefully vetting leaders for soft skill qualities such as integrity, empathy, humility, and altruism (in addition to ensuring they have the right competencies and technical skills for the role), we might just actually reduce the frequency of inappropriate workplace behaviors.

Using my own experience as an example, *Harasshole*, as I shared with the CEO immediately after interviewing him, had the competencies needed for the role. His other behaviors, however, were an indicator of his challenge with soft skills. Even knowing how to be appropriate during an interview. All of this should have been a huge red flag blowing violently in the wind. Maybe you are thinking he was just nervous? Nope, not a chance. His behavior with the CFO during that interview was also "off," according to what was shared with me directly by the CFO. A candidate who doesn't interact with the interviewer and DOES HIS EMAILS during an interview is a strong warning sign.

Research shows that toxic workers corrupt culture and inhibit the potential benefits that talented employees bring to the organization. This is only exacerbated when they are put in leadership roles. This is exactly what happened at my former employer.

There is a quote I've read that hits home for me: "You can tell a bully from a leader by how they treat people who disagree with them."

My former CEO = BULLY
Harasshole = BULLY

Just because you are smart or can get shit done doesn't make you a leader. We put too much emphasis on leaders. Just because someone isn't a good leader doesn't mean they aren't an asset. We often look at individual contributors as those who can't climb the ladder—we need to rethink this.

3. PROVIDE NEW AND TRUE CHANNELS FOR ANONYMOUS REPORTING

In today's environment, our employees don't expect most leaders to truly and honestly create an environment of open and transparent communication with their teams, where people feel the freedom to speak up and report harassment. Organizations must put in place other tools and processes that make anonymous reporting a "no risk" proposition to employees. Everyone has those anonymous help and tip lines to report behavior, and I suggested above that employees should use them. Do you know where ours went at my former employer? Hard wired to our legal counsel, even though it was an "anonymous" line. Culture of psychological safety—no way.

For all the bad press that surveillance tech gets, the bright side is that it can document and register offenses and protect those who report toxic behaviors. This is not just an HR problem but an organizational problem. For technology to help, leaders must be interested in helping, too, and not leveraging technology to simply identify those who are "troublemakers" for raising and reporting issues.

With COVID, so many employers are focused on using surveillance tech to monitor the hours people are working and their productivity. Trust is a two-way street. Do any of you HR people really think that one of your employees woke up this morning and decreed that they would intentionally become a problem for the company by reporting harassment? C'mon.

You would think that with remote work, incidents of harassment and bullying would decrease, as there's no physical environment in which to practice these activities, right? Statistics show just the opposite. It's flying under the radar because it's more private. For example, I know someone who started a new job and has yet to meet her colleagues in person. On multiple occasions, when she arrived to a Zoom call early, a male member of the executive team at her organization made comments like, "Oh, you put on makeup today." Please help me to understand why that is either appropriate or relevant. But she's in a situation where she's new-ish, and doesn't really know anyone at her new organization... what's she supposed to do? Not having an environment where one might get caught only exacerbates in some cases what people feel they can get away with.

4. INCENTIVIZE AND PROTECT PEOPLE WHO SPEAK UP

It's not reasonable to expect the majority of employees to display outstanding moral courage and risk their own careers by speaking up-- employers need to offer serious protection and even incentives for people to help improve their cultures from the bottom-up. Policy and processes follow the ethics and ethos of a company. They are the basic rules that determine whether the norm is a culture of integrity or a parasitic and corrupt culture. But they also reflect what is in place to begin with.

This is a bit of a radical idea, but as the saying goes, if nothing changes, nothing changes. It's quite obvious we need change, or these issues wouldn't continue to surface. This tactic gets coupled with the first one: creating an environment of psychological safety. We're starting to talk about brand safety which is discretely the goal of protecting the image and reputation of brands from negative or harmful influence via association with questionable or inappropriate content when advertising. We employ public relations resources who carry the mandate of reputation management, yet do we fear protecting our very own house from those inside who willingly light a match to see what will burn? The ones who yell "FIRE" are those who pay the price.

Let's get creative. This is not pay-for-play, or let's see how many incidents we can come up with, but rather about truly *creating* a culture of accountability where people will speak up and know that they are protected.

5. TAKE ACTION WHEN INAPPROPRIATE BEHAVIOR IS REPORTED

Every organization for whom I've worked or spoken with says they do this; however most don't until they have to. Employers need to be quicker to investigate, coach, counsel, and when warranted, not be afraid to remove the person who has behaved in an unprofessional manner. If you want people to feel safe at work, you need to take their well-being seriously. This includes properly investigating, holding people accountable for inappropriate behaviors, and taking action against offenders. In my *Harasshole's* case, there were multiple reports of inappropriate behavior from males and females across various functions. He displayed poor behavior right in front of the COO, his peers, his boss, and the CEO. There was no accountability, no action taken. He was promoted, and at the very end, allowed to walk with a package towards his next opportunity where he'll surely do this again.

I wish there were an HR Safety Net to catch such behavior. You, as Human Resources and Talent Acquisition professionals, have no way of knowing if your candidate has been a *Harasshole*. It doesn't show up on a background check. His/her references are those provided to you by the candidate, and the law prohibits former employees from disclosing much beyond a confirmation of employment, the dates, and possibly rehire eligibility.

Some companies will score big if they can figure this one out.

It's critical for both business leaders—and employees at all levels—to believe in and commit to the potential of workplaces around the world to behave the right way. It's discouraging that the conclusion reached by so many is that no company can be trusted, no company is worth commitment or putting yourself at risk. We should want people, our employees, to believe in the potential of employers to create great places to work that are free of inappropriate behavior. Workplaces where they can confidently and safely show up to do that which they are supposed to, their jobs.

6. CONDUCT BYSTANDER INTERVENTION TRAINING

This is training built on the premise that we all play a role in creating a safer space for each other when we see someone facing bias, discrimination, or harassment. Roll out tools and strategies to allow people to safely respond when they witness an incident that puts both the employee and company at risk. Equip your teams with verbal and behavioral de-escalation strategies to non-physically intervene or to disrupt unacceptable behavior. When you teach this, employees will learn how to become an effective ally, understand what safety means, and acknowledge that everyone has a role to play in creating a safer environment. Bowman's POV only—this is something we should teach in schools. I guarantee you my *Harasshole* terrorized the girls in his class while in school.

There are companies and non-profits emerging that specialize in this training. It's the intelligent companion piece to the anti-harassment and discrimination training that companies invest countless hours and dollars of lost productivity in deploying. Employees learn what's not okay, but beyond contacting HR, whom they often don't trust, they aren't really trained on what to do.

7. ESTABLISH AN INDEPENDENT COUNCIL TO HEAR COMPLAINTS

The value of an outside counsel or ombudsmen cannot be overstated. Boards are not responsible for fulfilling this role, rather, they have a fiduciary responsibility to the organization. In my case, when my former employer conducted an "investigation" as a response to the media coverage, they never spoke to the three of us who had all filed EEOC charges within a one-year period.

A group of 20+ former women employees who had all had the same experience during their tenure wrote to the board—they offered to talk. The board rejected that, too. Folks, where there is smoke, there is fire. Multiple EEOC claims for the same behavior with the same person are flashing red lights. Multiple EEOC claims for the same organization-also a red flag.

Not to drag politics into this, but even Facebook established a completely independent council to evaluate the ban on Trump and whether it should be upheld in perpetuity. A council of independent experts who can listen to complaints objectively and make a recommendation to leadership as to whether or not there's a "there there" can be invaluable.

Given the lack of trust between employees and employer, an independent counsel who doesn't know the employee, doesn't have their judgment potentially influenced or colored by ancillary issues or opinions hold much value as a new approach to an old problem.

8. NON-DISCLOSURE AGREEMENTS (NDA) FOR IP ONLY

Non-disclosure agreements serve as a tool of silence. They're used to hide poor behavior, and they truly don't keep people from talking. If you have nothing to hide, you should only need an NDA to protect your IP.

When individuals give up on institutions, we're all at enormous risk of falling into a vicious cycle of cynicism that results in each of us focusing solely on taking care of oneself–and letting others do likewise.

When too many people think this way, society as we know it, for better or worse, begins to collapse.

And by extension, when employees stop caring about their companies, they also start to care less about their customers. If no one owes anything to anyone, it's not just employee beware, but also employer beware and buyer beware. Each one for himself. Worse, if one never cares, one is no longer obligated to speak up against inappropriate behavior.

Please don't conclude that speaking up isn't worthwhile, but rather, resolve to work harder to hire and retain people who live up to the organization's values and standards. Hire and train upstanders instead of accepting bystanders. We'll all be better for it, I promise. We're all familiar with SaaS, software as a service. Shouldn't executives also be looking at LaaS (Leadership as a Service) for the organization and its employees? As a marketer, I'm expected to focus on customer experience, but employee experience is just as critical. You can't have external-facing policies and values to flaunt to the public if you're not taking care of business properly inside the house. Otherwise, when a story like mine breaks, your credibility goes to hell. And if your employees don't believe you, why would your customers?

In closing, my hope and wish for the next generations is that they encounter a workplace that is free of the challenges we face today because we've realized it's time to turn #MeToo into an old hashtag that is nothing more than a historic relic we used to use.

I'm all in. Are you?

> "And once you realize that you can do something, it would be difficult to live with yourself if you didn't do it."
> James Baldwin

Acknowledgements

Archer for all of the support and propping me up when I needed it, dealing with "zoom-zoom-zip-zip and LEVEL 20," making me say "yes" and until ninety plus; Mom and Dad—I hope you'd be proud—thanks for raising me the way you did; Brenda for taking good care of Dad. Gram for sharing your wisdom; Jason, always family; Sid and Adele for the many, many years of friendship and support; Kettle for being my ride or die on this one; The "UW 20+" including AJP, LP, KB, JN, and the rest, thanks for your bravery in stepping up and speaking out; Ana for your fearlessness; Angela my sister from another mister and F-Bomb Queen; Jamie Robinson for making me come to New York in March of 2020; Kathleen Butcher for building my strength even when I felt weak; Gretchen Carlson for responding to my email and everything else. Emily Peck and Yelena Dzhanova for helping tell my story; Lan Phan for your huge heart and selflessness—you inspire me more than you'll ever know; Georgina Salguero for teaching me how to throw plates and gifting me the lost art of old-fashioned letter writing; Victoria Rumsey for just being you all this time; The Gentlewoman Boss, The Omaha Oracle, and Chelsey G for confirming it's not just me—keep fighting;

David Abney for "coffee talk" and your support; All of the UPSers who reached out to me in support and stopped their donations to United Way—always Brown; Community of 7 CORE 1 for always lifting each other up; Cath Weitnauer for "cautionary tales" and years of friendship; Loren; Kenan—my funny friend, for the laughter, the lift ups, and Kenan-tinis always; Christine Davis for always making me feel like I helped while walking; Adrienne Wallace for teaching me about being powHERful by owning their names—Namaste; KIP for your friendship always and being a member of the Supastar Fan Club; Tracy Avin for the opportunity to give voice to this via Troop; AllieJack, for all the light and love sent my way; Russ Klein and the AMA Board for your support, kindness and caring during this process; Ted Wright for giving me a kick in the ass to step out there; Kevin S for thinking Wonder Woman is a Superhero and confusing me with her; Elisa P. for being new friends but definitely friends; Michael and Amy Port for teaching me the way; Tamer for your help; those on the "inside" who kept me apprised and fought for me silently—thank you for taking the risk; The local United Way CEOs who stood up for what's right—thank you, things should be better in your world now, too; Mojo for keeping me company throughout. Teresa for being a good person with crystal clear vision. Sof-I knew #youtoo; Bob Lambert for being a sounding board. Ron and Cigdem for pushing me to do what I thought I couldn't; Curtis Key for shaping this; Others who have supported me or stood by me on this journey whom I may have omitted unintentionally—know that I appreciate each and every person who has touched my life or stood by me during this. THANK YOU, ALL.

And finally, *Harasshole* and BAG, you didn't break me even though you tried; I'm stronger than I knew.

EPILOGUE

"When They Go Low, We Go High"
Michelle Obama

Literally, as we were going to press on this book in the last week of 2021, United Way came to the table with a "settlement offer". Once my two years of legal fees and the bonus they withheld were subtracted, it amounted to what they should have offered me as severance before 24 months of emotional duress. As a matter of fact, it was very close to the amount my attorney countered with at the time of my separation.

Suspicious timing, right? I'll say it's a safe assumption they knew this book was coming. There is new leadership in place. Female. I don't know the new CEO; she wasn't a party to this and candidly until this point, I bore her no ill-will. By accepting the offer in principle, I extended an olive branch to her in the spirit of providing closure and allowing her to do what she needed to restore the organization without the shadow of "this" hanging over them.

As is standard practice in most settlement agreements that are essentially a template of standard legalese and "insert dollar figure + payment terms HERE", this one was no exception. It contained a standard clause of no admission of wrong doing by the organization. It required me to withdraw the complaint from the Equal Employment

Opportunity Commission, essentially erasing any record of it existing. And of utmost importance, it contained language which would have silenced me from talking about what happened and prohibited the publication of this book.

I had to think about it. For about two seconds. Was it worth my taking what I should have received as severance to buy my silence? Did it make me complicit to some extent in covering this behavior? Yes, and no. The coverage from the HuffPost, Business Insider and other publications will live on forever on the web. I was shocked to find that there is now reference to me on the United Way Wikipedia page.

But the real story wasn't out there. Some of the facts were. But the media coverage didn't tell the journey of what really transpired. The emotional road down which I traveled. What to do should you find yourself in the same situation I was. So the resounding answer to staying silent, in the words of Randy Jackson on American Idol were, "it's a no for me, dawg".

We entered into negotiations. I even went so far as to offer to give the organization a lift by drafting an epilogue that asked you, the reader not to hold the actions of former employees against an entire organization. Honestly, I thought given the circumstances that was a very generous offer on my part given all I've been through. Which I NEVER should have been subjected to. And after two months of running up my legal bills under the pretense of a negotiation we got nowhere. They simply stopped responding as we were near agreement according to what was communicated by their attorney. The reason it fell apart? Given the timing, I can only surmise that it's because for what they offered, I would not agree to non-disclosure or confidentiality language that prohibited either this book or my ability to talk about my experience there. Initially, they agreed. However, with the last minute identification of a few slippery words intended protect me and take away their leverage to come after me for speaking the truth, they slid back into silence. I don't for one second believe this was initially or ever oriented in a good faith effort to get us there, it was the only thing they had to go after me on. So much for the rumored cultural change that was poised to abound with the new leadership.

This was never about the money for me; it was about justice and accountability.

I will own my experience vs. letting them buy my silence. The organization who fought me all along the way and who was suddenly concerned about the impact of this book on their reputation should have thought about that when they took no action on Harasshole and allowed this to become the event it did.

While we sat on hold waiting for this situation to play out, the EEOC contacted me and after two years is ready to begin processing my case by completing their third-party evaluation of the evidence submitted in the next few weeks. I remain confident that there will be a Determination of Cause in my favor. And when that happens, I'll take United Way to court and allow this to be settled through a legal process that remains broken, but it's what we have.

I've said it before and I'll say it again and again; "I would not have chosen this experience for anything, but perhaps it chose me."

My story will be out there and my conscience will be at peace. The journey continues as this has yet to be resolved. To stay informed or contact me, please visit www.harasshole.com

ABOUT THE AUTHOR

Lisa Bowman is a first-time author and long tenured "marchitect" who has built brands for global organizations such as UPS and United Way. She is currently the Chief Mojo Officer of Marketing Mojo.

   A self-admitted glamazon, Lisa believes there is nothing that can't be accomplished while wearing a good pair of heels. When faced with the injustice of retaliation that culminated in a wrongful termination for reporting sexual harassment, Lisa realized that her ability to navigate tough terrain in 5" heels was the platform that allowed her to stand up for herself and others. At least that's what her Twitter profile says.

   A native Chicagoan who never met a deep -dish pizza she didn't like, Lisa currently resides in Atlanta with her husband Bill and Alaskan Klee Kai rescue, Mojo.

   When not engaged in other activities, Lisa enjoys travel, working out and retail therapy.